You're The Answer To The Problem:

From the Hood to Harvard and Back Again

By Lewis W. Spears

Printed in the United States of America

2018 First Edition

10 9 8 7 6 5 4 3 2 1

Subject Index:

Spears, Lewis.

Title: You're The Answer to the Problem: From the Hood to Harvard and Back Again

1. Jersey City, New Jersey 2. Education 3. Rutgers University 4. Community 5. Black Males 6. Black Youth

Library of Congress Card Catalog Number: 2019901498

Paperback ISBN: 978-0-578-460666-6

Cover Photo Credit: Stephen Reid Stephen Reid, www.stephenreidphotography.com

AJ Publishing

website: www.thehoodtoharvard.com

A+ For The Best Answer...

"Lewis Spears has captured the true realities that most young Black men go through in life in this book - I can truly relate and so can the 87 boys in my school. Being a young Black man in South Africa, your journey is set up for failure by the system that has been created by the Apartheid era and when you succeed, it is seen as a miracle. Lewis clearly points it out that we are also programmed to believe that we as Black men are not meant to succeed by our townships (hoods).

You're the Answer to the Problem, gives a solution to many issues that young Black men can relate to and deep insight into what went wrong in most societies. One fact that is also made very clear in the book is that the problems that are in our townships (Hoods) are there for us to solve. It is a guide to true introspection and awareness for men in today's generation."

James Malope
Principal (Headmaster)
LEAP Science and Maths School, South Africa

"The human experience is a complex, and often winding journey of self-discovery, healing, agency, and self-realization. *You're the Answer to the Problem: From the Hood to Harvard*

iii

and Back Again, is an intimate and transparent story of a man's transformative experience of examining his own life to find purpose, understanding, and most importantly, compassion and empathy for himself. Lewis Spears uses stories and examples from his life, coupled with conceptual applications from Mathematics, to impart wisdom to his readers about how Black and brown boys can transcend their circumstances. As a Black woman who walked the path from the "hood" to realizing my own purpose, it was gaining the understanding that life is not happening to you but you to it that ultimately changed the trajectory of my life. This book is a tool to help its readers to apply this philosophical concept to real life and step into their greatness."

Dr. Ayanna S. Kersey-McMullen, DO, MSPH

"You're the Answer to the Problem, is a pivotal message to young Black and brown males today, that they have the power to be the change that they want to see. With so many negative statistics on the plight of these young men with regard to high incarceration rates, gang affiliations, drugs, and violence, Lewis offers his life story as a perfect illustration that they can also turn the negative statistics into positive, life-changing outcomes. His book is a must-read message of hope, empowerment, and paying it forward."

Dr. Alex Ellis
Founder, Tied To Greatness

"As a fellow alumnus of Booker T. Washington Projects in Jersey City, New Jersey, I am honored to share in my brother's journey as a graduate of "the school of hard knocks." Lewis' transparency growing up in the hood despite dysfunction all around him, to becoming a college graduate, husband, father, and then the Ivy League is a testament to his character. His determination not to succumb to the negative forces of his environment resonates on so many levels that our youth face today. **You're the Answer**, is a message of hope and empowerment to young Black men and challenges them to change the tragic narratives in their community. Lewis' return to his hometown is a prime example of one man being the change that he wants to see. It starts with one person, one community at a time."

President/C.E.O
Coley Mustafa Speaks Enterprises, Inc.

"You're the Answer to the Problem: From the Hood to Harvard and Back Again, is a poignant and much needed autobiographical account of how one man was able to face adversity and beat the odds to accomplish so much in such a brief period of time. Written by someone that so many young Black men relate to, Lewis Spears book is one that's educational, empowering and enlightening. As an educator and counselor who works with kids from the hood and as a product of Trenton, NJ myself, I highly recommend it as required reading for young urban males to show them

that they too can dare to dream bigger and actualize their greatest potential. It also serves a learning tool for educators to offer them insight on what educators of young males from urban areas are struggling with and how they can serve as a resource to them. Thank you, Lewis, for being willing to share your testimony to remind others that their location doesn't determine their destination."

Reggie Walker
Educator/Author/Counselor

"This is merely the literary trailer before the blockbuster hit! I consider this work the *Chicken Noodle Soup* for the ghetto soul, the hood intellect, and their parents. Spears speaks of generational curses, the impact that double consciousness has on the Black man and yet still infuses a sense of hope, gratitude, and validation. As an African- American school leader and former English teacher, this is the type of literature needed in classrooms to build upon the cultural capital that our Black and brown babies already bring into the school building. *You're The Answer to the Problem* is needed to guide the professional development of teachers who choose to teach our Black and brown babies."

Shavonne M. McMillan, M.Ed.
Middle School Principal

"Lewis is an agent of change and has worked tirelessly to empower others to challenge the systemic hurdles in our

communities. In a game with life or death consequences that are so often designed for us to fail, Lewis' book provides a blueprint not just for survival but for success."
James Alexander Lewis, V, Esq.
Partner, Pennington Law Group

"In urban cities, people create myths that if you are able to jump high, dribble a ball, run fast and score touchdowns, or be able to rap -that is your ticket to be successful or "to get out of the hood." Lewis breaks all misconceptions and myths by demonstrating that there are other avenues to overcome all obstacles and be successful. Lewis Spears takes readers on an authentic, heartfelt, and inspiring journey of peaks and valleys. Lewis couldn't control the cards he was dealt in life, but he sure knew how to play them. This book brings the message that your situation doesn't determine your destination. It is a must read! Congratulations!"
Carlos Perez
Senior Pastor, COGOP Newark Church
Principal, Jersey City Public Schools

"I'm awed at how Lewis was able to magnify the journey of the Black man/boy through the lens of physical abuse, mental abuse, sexual abuse, poverty, death, education, and love. Lewis's life speaks to the saying, 'your present situation is not your final destination.' A must read for all who aspire to be GREAT!"
Eric Rhett Jr.
Black Entertainment Television (BET)

"By sharing the challenges, pitfalls, and pain of his own journey in such vivid detail, Lewis Spears has provided us all with a simply beautiful formula for success in life - Believing you can and knowing you are good enough. *You're The Answer To The Problem* is an uplifting must-read for all dreamers and visionaries seeking to make positive, inclusive change happen in their communities."

Gillian Sarjeant-Allen,
President, Black Wall Street Jersey City

"One of the best speakers I have come across in my travels has put together a written masterpiece that serves as a roadmap for our youth. With the paucity of a good example of men, Lewis serves as that for the youth that he serves. By sharing his journeys, being vulnerable, and giving his keys to success makes this book a must read for all ages even for college students and grown men. I know for a fact that anyone who picks this book up will not regret it and will be led to share it with others, an engaging read that I am sure we will refer to decades from now. You're the answer is more than the answer for our generation, it is the GPS to destiny for the youth."

Michael Spence
Youth Pastor & Motivational Speaker

"Lewis uses this transformative piece to take readers through his journey to "purpose" and shines a light on unspoken roadblocks we must begin to acknowledge about our Black and brown boys in the inner city. Mr. Spears helps us all to be more self-reflective and forces us to change the stereotypes we carry about ourselves and our Black and brown boys. His life is a testimony and through this candid piece, I believe he will encourage our community and those invested in it, to do better, be better and never settle for our beginnings to dictate our endings."

Sharmonique Henry
Author, Marketing & Sales Executive

"**You're the Answer to the Problem**, offers a transparent view into Lewis' life as a young man determined to succeed despite the challenges at home and a negative community environment. Just like Lewis, readers are encouraged to see themselves as agents of change to transform their communities for the better. Lewis has journeyed back to his hometown of Jersey City, New Jersey to transform the very neighborhood he grew up in. He has come full circle and daily exemplifies what is needed for other young men and women to overcome the hurdles in their own life. He is destined to make a lasting impact in the state and in the nation by utilizing all that he has learned in college, at Harvard, and teaching in urban communities. Everyone who reads this book will get something out of it. Lewis is a shining example of the African-American proverb, each one teach one."

David Carment
Lead Pastor and church planter of Greenville Church
and community partner with Lewis Spears in Jersey City

"Lewis Spears' candor and transparency of his journey and experiences are truly inspiring. He is a living example of how grit and perseverance afford the answers to your problems."

Brigitte Beauvoir
Executive Director with Charlotte-Mecklenburg School

"Inspiringly enthralling! Fueled by a tenacious passion for world-changing, **You're the Answer to the Problem** ignites an awakening fire within the reader's spirit! Through a courageously candid account of his hope-filled hood to Harvard story, intertwined with applicable advisement and savvy solutions, Mr. Spears saturates the pages with life success formulas. Fragranced with relatability, *You're the Answer* is a must-read for anyone who aspires to be a vehicle of change in addressing the unique struggles of Black and brown boys hailing from a lower socioeconomic background."

Alisa French
Teacher, Jersey City Public Schools District

"To know Lewis Spears is to be inspired. His story, his zest for life, his ability to connect with people, young and old, from all walks of life, is as inspiring as it is unique. I've had the great privilege to know and to learn from Lewis for the last decade. This book is recommended reading for anyone who wants to do the same."

John Glennon Jr.
Headmaster, Georgetown Preparatory School

DEDICATION

To the purest longitudinal relationship that I will ever have on this side of the Earth, Myriam, I love you. I am because YOU are. With me, the ride of life is going to be excitingly adventurous, I warned you years ago; too bad you are stuck now!

To my beautiful baby boy, AJ! Your acute sense of awareness makes me want to create a world that you're comfortable to freely engage. My love for you allows me to see the true essence of having a purpose-driven life. We love you very much.

To my creators, Regina and Lewis, two very complex, yet simple individuals who decided to dote on your son. Mom, thanks for your sacrifice! Your wisdom is unmatched and your love knows no limits. I love you. I can hear you now, "Don't take no wooden nickels." I promise you will never have to worry about that! Dad, thanks for getting out of your way long enough to have me build a genuine connection with you. I'm grateful for the love you have shown me.

TABLE OF CONTENTS

"Success is to be measured not so much by the position that one has reached in life as by the obstacles which he has overcome."

– Booker T. Washington

Booker T. Washington Projects, Jersey City, NJ

PREFACE

"Black success should not be an anomaly."

The revelations began once I arrived on the campus of Rutgers University in June of 2005 as a product of the Educational Opportunity Fund (EOF) Program. Still in my first year, it was my second semester of history class. I was one of six Black students and approximately 40 white students in attendance. On this particular chilly Spring morning, for some reason, I looked around to see if my peers could relate to any of my experiences growing up in the hood. We had been talking about dysfunctional families for the past few weeks. The discussions were very interesting and disturbing at the same time. As I listened to the silver-haired, white male professor in his 60's, standing in front of the classroom, I felt a weird sensation in the back of my neck. I put my elbow on the desk and grabbed my neck, and looked down at my lap to ensure I did not make eye contact. I was surprised that my tiny neck-hairs were standing at full attention.

By now the professor had made one full lap across the room. With his left hand in the pocket of his khakis, and trademark navy sweater vest, he swayed as he spoke. He went on to explain the attributes of dysfunction, including one or more family members being addicted to drugs or alcohol, constant household conflict, unpredictability, instability and physical, verbal, emotional or sexual abuse. In all, the sum total of daily drama.

Then, it hit me like a ton of bricks! *Dude, the Spears family is dysfunctional!* I thought to myself. Of course, I had a general understanding of what dysfunction meant, but there was never a label or judgment connected to it as it related to my upbringing. In my mind, it was always, *"Man, my mom's crazy!"* I began to fidget in my seat. My palms got cold, yet the rest of my body felt warmer than usual. I tried to gauge the facial expressions and body language of two Black students within my view. Either they were great poker players or they just never experienced *any* type of dysfunction in their lives. Totally blank. I tilted my head down and stared at my desk. *I can't be the only one*, I whispered.

All of a sudden, the feeling of not being good enough crept inside. My next reaction to the professor's lecture was to become defensive. He had no idea that his comments and analysis were hitting home concerning my chaotic upbringing in the Booker T. Projects, in Jersey City - the hood. I really wanted to raise my hand and say, "Me and my neighbors were borrowing sugar from each other a few times a week. You can never have enough sugar to make Kool-Aid," or better yet, "After a drunken fight, between my neighbors and my family, everyone still loved each other the next day." I felt conflicted because I wanted to weigh in on my reality, yet I was too embarrassed to comment. I had hundreds of stories to fill each criterion.

I later learned about Survivor's Remorse, where the "surviving" member has to be responsible (financially) for the rest of the family. The professor also spoke about irresponsible behaviors like paying for sneakers or other ancillary services before taking care of the primary needs of a family. I identified with that because there were several times our lights were cut off, but we kept up with the Jones' and had the latest outfit or gadget.

Sitting in history class on that Tuesday morning was the first time I felt disenfranchised. It was like I didn't qualify to be there. I heard it in the pitch of people's voices when they questioned me with the sound of surprise, "You, go to Rutgers?" I didn't understand what the big deal was. My response was simple: "Yeah, I applied and got in!" However, on that day, this history class lecture created an urgent desire for me to re-examine my life. In hindsight, I consider that classroom experience in Spring 2006, my first "woke" moment.

As a young Black male growing up in Jersey City, New Jersey, I wasn't supposed to be successful. Obviously, the definition of success varies from person-to-person, but society tends to measure it in dollars and tangible possessions. In the hood, male success could be defined as being 17 years old and never been locked up or a hustler. Truthfully, not being shot is also high on the list of achievements. Therefore, finishing high school *and* college is definitely a successful accomplishment on many levels, but such a feat was not even on the radar in my community.

Amongst my peers, the common blueprint for a kid in the projects starts out being raised by a single mother on welfare with limited education. As the kid gets older, he becomes ingrained with a misinformed symbolic street cred of his future: drug dealer, drug addict, bum, stick-up kid, streetballer, locked up or dead. Any other aspirations that a young man like myself had of a positive future would have to take a back seat to overall survival. I am bothered that this outlook has been the norm for young Black men in the hood for too long. This dynamic is both a generational and historical tragedy.

Many people inside and outside of my hood see the fact that I became successful in spite of my upbringing, as an anomaly; both spoken and unspoken. "It's-a-great-thing-you-made-it-out!" resonates as false accolades in an environment where people live "by any means necessary." *Why was I one of the few who made it out?* I've asked myself that question numerous times. *What made me different?* I was outgoing, charismatic and had a knack for building relationships and working with people. I was very task-oriented and goal-driven at an early age. Another one of my strong points was that I had the ability to create something out of nothing.

When you think about it, if the scenario described a white boy in a white community, the "anomaly" would be that he's a deadbeat or "will never amount to anything." I want to bring attention to the biased societal lens and show the disparity between the odds of a young Black boy becoming successful, versus the optimistic future outlook of the young Caucasian male.

"We are tied together in the single garment of destiny, caught in an inescapable network of mutuality. And whatever affects one directly affects all indirectly."
- Dr. Martin Luther King Jr.

I hope to demonstrate how our Black boys are set up for failure because of the images displayed in the media, as well as the ill-informed expectations that are placed upon them, especially when it comes to making money, being irresponsible, and taking advantage of women. I want to help bridge the gap and provide love and acceptance to young Black men who have been abandoned by their families, the system, and society at large. Each of us that have "made it" should play a part in bringing our young brothers up to help them navigate more positive paths in life.

Although I don't agree, I can see why the white male glorifies his success as a means to justify racism, when he proudly states, "I'm not a racist. There is a system in which hard work equals success!" It pains me when I think about why this "equal work system" is not accessible to those in my community, and if it was, then we all would have a better chance of making it out. I've worked hard for my success as an educator in various math disciplines, and educational leadership, and I am working even harder to give back to underserved communities.

This book has been pressing in my heart and spirit for a few years. I have found that by being intentional and perceptively woke, I can positively influence the lives of young people and present them with a realistic plan, as well as hope for a better future. One of my favorite math topics has always been Geometry. It's one of those subjects where you have to understand the congruence and similarity of properties often, very much the same way in life. Almost like in the children's picture book, *Math Curse*, which illustrates how math literally plays an aspect in several areas of our daily lives without realizing it. Even if we take the numbers out of the equation, the definitions and concepts from a relational perspective are clear and relevant.

As you will see, there are several math-related concepts and metaphors to explain key points in my life, as well as to tap into those "wake up call" situations to help readers make changes in their lives. There are eight chapters. Even though seven is the number of completion, eight represents my return to my community and new beginnings. I believe there is a recipe for mentoring and connecting people, regardless of where you are from or where you currently live. I want to be that example, the guinea pig so to speak, for high school and college students, parents, teachers, and administrators, that despite the lack of a fruitful pedigree, young Black men can succeed in STEM fields or any field they desire.

I have no problem standing in the mirror to offer readers a candid, transparent view of my circumstances, and use my life and these formulas as a vehicle to help you achieve your dreams. No matter what you have been through, as long as you have breath, your dreams are valid and can be lived out fearlessly. Stay positive. Remain focused. Be diligent. Ask questions. Seek mentors. Your future self is waiting for you to step into your destiny. You're the answer to solving the problems in your hood and in society. Believe in yourself, start in your neighborhood, and together we can make positive, radical changes one hood at a time.

1st Marking Period

THE HOOD: Life Lessons/ Survival of the Fittest

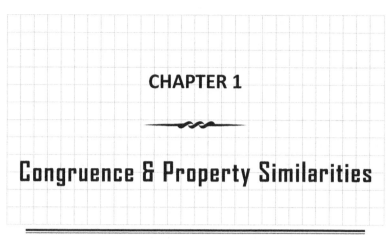

CHAPTER 1

Congruence & Property Similarities

> "The imprint of the father remains
> forever on the life of a child."
>
> **Roy Lessin**

A Letter To My Dad

Date: January 23, 2016

Dear Lewis:

I pretty much hate you for everything. How are you going to have a kid and not even give him your last name? So what if we have the same first name. I am not a junior! Why did you do that? Why didn't you take me anywhere? Like for Christmas, first birthday that I can remember or life in general. You didn't think of it? It's not important to you? Did you ever think about me? Who you thought was going to teach me how to be a man? My mom? My grandma? My aunties? I guess you didn't even care! You weren't there, but yet you criticized me

3

for who I was to other people. For a second, I almost felt sorry for you that you could not see the difference between me and all the other kids in the hood. I was focused. I was serious about school. Serious about my future.

So guess what? Your focused son doesn't love you either! I had to learn everything that a man is supposed to do on my own. How could you not be there for me? I feel disposable like you just threw me away. Do you not see what everybody else sees in me? Why is it that teachers and other adults say that I'm great and everyone gives me a bunch of accolades, but you just ran away from me? You neglected me. You left me hanging. Did anyone ever tell you that my stepdad abused me from time-to-time because he didn't like the way I did things? Where were you to protect me? I wanted you to say that no matter what happens to me in life, that you were going to be there to pick me up.

I had to depend on the rest of your family to take care of me. I see how you took care of Desmond and the other two girls. He ain't even your son! He's your girlfriend's son, but he gets to have you on his birthday and Christmas. Desmond gets to stay up and watch movies with you. He gets to do all the things that I saw my brother doing with his dad. I just don't feel good enough. I don't feel like you love me. Why? I'm short like you. I have your smile. I have your charisma. So, what's not to like about me? Why can't I have you?

Guess what? Things that you say get back to me. Interestingly enough, you brag to your friends about all of my accomplishments as if you assisted in helping me to be the person that I am. I would argue to say that your neglect actually took it away. There's no way that when I become a dad that I would desert or make any of my kids feel that they are not a part of me, like I don't value them. It's scary because I went to other men in the community to really build me up. Some of them had done a really good job like my cousin Sean, Mr. Kabili and Alfonso. I needed you, but you were nowhere around.

I swear, if you died today, I would not even go to your funeral. You will be lucky if I didn't spit on your grave! As a matter of fact, why don't you die? What purpose do you serve? When I call you and ask for things, your response is that I only call when I need something, or you remind me that I get child support. The point is that at least I call you. That little $50 a month does nothing for me. I have learned that I have to work to make it in this world. I also learned that I have to work even harder for you to notice me. Wow. Extremely disappointed.

Signed: Your Real Son, Lewis Spears Morrison

This letter was written *four* years after his passing. My therapist suggested that I write a letter to each of my parents and myself. No, I am not ashamed of going to a therapist. When I think about it, besides asking my wife Myriam to marry me, therapy is one of the best that decisions I have ever made. The letter came from the feeling that I was never good enough and it was from the heart after years of neglect. I struggled with low self-esteem for many years. Now, I can honestly say that this is not an issue for me, but like most of us, there are challenges to functioning productively each day. Even though my parents did not validate me, and maybe your parents failed in this area as well, you should know that you are more than enough.

Thinking back, there were job opportunities that I passed up. I rehearsed a very short bio so that I did not have to reveal too much about me. I missed investment opportunities, networking opportunities and opportunities for personal growth. I was in the shadows watching my dad enjoying his own life with their daughter and her other kids. He never reached out to help my mom when our lights were being cut off, which happened often or on those occasions where we regularly did without. My negative self-esteem was a byproduct of my environment. I was this hindrance in the middle of two men who were supposed to look out for me and teach me how to be a man. Instead, my dad wanted nothing to do with me and Kenny, my stepdad did not accept me for who I was.

I fit Kenny's stereotype as this northerner kid reading all these books and instructing him how to pronounce words. He often shouted at me for being smart. It's funny, in the hood if you are not a hardcore knucklehead or troublemaker, you were not considered a *real* man. I wanted my dad Lewis to stand up for me to Kenny so badly, but he never did. I saw daily sacrifices from my mom and in my mind, that equated to me being of less value to him. **Lewis left me susceptible to**

any bad things that were happening to me, even in my own household.

Mirror Mirror

When I was younger, the proximity of my apartment and my father Lewis' apartment puzzled me. *How could there be no real connection?* Lewis lived in the Lafayette PJ's, which were directly across the street from my family in Booker T. Any meetings that I had with him were merely coincidental. It was a bit weird running into him, yet, I didn't feel like I was missing out on anything since most of my friends were fatherless like me. Oftentimes I convinced myself that Lewis' absence came down to him assuming that Kenny would take care of me the same way he was taking care of his girlfriend's son. When I walked down the street, someone would shout, "That's your dad over there," pointing in his direction. If we were in the same grocery store, he would introduce me to a third party and say, "Yeah, this is my son." Everyone who knew my dad called me "Little Lewis." One evening I spent the night with him and his girlfriend and I felt so uncomfortable. I really liked his girlfriend, but staying under her roof with Lewis and three other kids was weird. I vowed to never sleep over again.

Lewis dressed homely and wore jeans, T-shirt and shoes. He was very plain and in the summer sported socks with sandals. He drove the short school buses, was a Teacher's Assistant, and worked with kids his entire life. *Hey, what about your kid across the street?* He took pride in his job and made about $120 each week. Towards the end of high school, my accolades were recognized in the local newspapers. Articles were written about my memberships in various clubs and teachers and community leaders were saying great things about me. I was in a chariot in a parade for winning an award. My aunt saw me and told Lewis about it. She said he smiled and seemed pleased. I guess in his eyes he knew he had an amazing son. Who knows, maybe he decided to fall back because he felt he could not compete with me? Now that I was coming into manhood, I thought this was the best time for him to just be there for me.

Then, the girlfriend whom I had come to know and love, decided to move on after 12 years together. My dad Lewis was unable to work because of a poor heart condition. He was in and out of the hospital so he had to stay home to collect disability and live that out to qualify for government assistance. He eventually lost his place and moved in with his brother who was a military veteran. His brother was dying and needed round the clock care. Lewis was there for his brother.

Lewis started inviting me to his talk of the town BBQ's. To give you a snapshot of the type of person my dad was, he gave an annual cookout in the Lafayette housing complex with free food and drink for everyone in attendance. People from different walks of life simply came by for a bite to eat. He was constantly open to friends, telling jokes and having fun. I wondered where I got my jovial side from, and it was evident that I retrieved that aspect of my personality from him. I loved seeing him interact with his friends, many of whom I perceived to be down on their luck, yet he treated each one with respect; even the skinny guy with a limp. Which is what everyone called him, as he was known by his deficiency. The skinny guy talked slowly and the aftermath of a stroke caused him to walk with a limp. There was no stratification in how Lewis treated his friends. I learned from that very short, yet enlightening experience, that it was OK to love everyone and ultimately treat everyone the same despite their background.

After that cookout, I was able to walk in complete authority with my newfound self! My eventual relationship with my dad was vital for my optimal growth. It was the first time that I looked into a mirror and actually liked what I saw. We were finally forming a sincere relationship. Wow! I thought, *how could this amazingly friendly, well-respected man who was loved by his community, be able to take care in many aspects, his friends, but abandon his only biological son?* I began to create all types of excuses on his behalf. Even ones that villainized my mother, the one person who gave up her entire life to raise me, and I might add, she has done a great job! I couldn't fathom my dad just simply not wanting to be part of my life. Especially now that I was a college student.

I thought there had to be a legitimate reason why he didn't want to be around me. I never really put the responsibility on him because I imagined there was this justifiably, gargantuan reason that he was OK neglecting his responsibilities as a

9

dad. As I stated earlier, I saw a mirror, and in there I projected his actions onto myself and tried to put myself in his shoes. That's when I realized that he did the best with what he knew how to do. We all did. I am sure that he could have done better. Yet given the tools, he had produced all that he could. I saw that me judging him would not have changed a thing.

However, if I began to provide sympathy and compassion to understand where he was coming from, then I could ultimately get through the day. As I was learning more about the plight of the Black man in America, knowing that it was not easy for him as he was struggling with his own insecurities, as well as psychological and physical ailments. In hindsight, what if your dad's sole purpose was just to bring you here? Now that you're here, it's up to you to make something of yourself, without his help, but with the help of others strategically placed in your life. I don't believe that my father had the skills to raise me to be the man that I am today. So I sleep better at night knowing that there was a purpose behind it all.

I had a hard time calling a man "Dad." I called my grandfather "granddaddy," and even questioned that title at some point because he used to beat on my grandma. I called my father "Lewis" because he wasn't always around. I called my stepdad "Kenny" because he didn't take responsibility for me. Neither of these men was worthy to be addressed as *my dad*. I realize that many people would say, "Lewis, at least you grew up with a stepdad in the house." Agreed. But since I wasn't his biological son, my stepdad Kenny could not validate me in my personality struggles which were difficult for me. Yet, when I got older and was around my dad, Lewis, I felt confident in being who I was because I saw myself in him and I saw him for who he was, nothing more, nothing less.

360 Degree Turnaround

For my wedding in 2010, I said, to my dad "Dude you are wearing a tuxedo!" He came through for me. He rented a Black tuxedo and looked really nice. I watched him beam with pride as he sat on the first-row corner seat. When I entered the sanctuary, he was the first person I saw on my right side. I was filled with excitement. After the pastor said, "I now pronounce you husband and wife," I immediately gave him a high five. It was a moment where time stood still for me and I am grateful for that.

Without a doubt, I inherited my love of people from him. Despite not having a relationship with Lewis for my childhood and teenage years, I connected with my paternal bloodline through my older cousin, Sean, my dad's nephew who worked in Marion's Barber Shop, on Pacific Avenue. Sean always made sure that I had a fresh cut. He looked out for me and bought me things like shoes and clothes. He even paid for my Military Ball outfit. Sean was truly the first man to love me unconditionally. Other males in my family could not relate to me for the most part. I felt like I was always treated differently. They knew that I was different since I did not hang out and do the mischievous things that my other cousins did.

Instead, I was comfortable sitting outside on the bench listening to adult conversations.

Marion's Barber Shop

When I first started getting haircuts my stepdad had a friend, Derrick who was a known drug user make house calls. Kayvon and I sat around the house waiting for him to come. When he arrived, he set up things in the living room. Derrick would put a cape around Kayvon and me and cut our hair. Mom did not like it because he always gave us a rough cut. Even though my stepdad paid him, it never looked like we went to a barber. I crossed paths with Derrick several times a few years later when I was in the 5th grade since he was dating the mother of my first girlfriend, Alison.

As a young man, the impact of going to a Black barbershop gave me a sense of community and inclusion. The barbershop experience is something that we all go through as young men and old men. Getting my haircut by my cousin Sean was my first time in a real barbershop. I looked forward to sitting in there waiting for my turn in Sean's chair. My ears were glued to every conversation from sports to politics to women.

I found it interesting how these adult conversations went from playing the dozens to each other's haircuts or style of clothes. Not to mention that there was always a sports argument. My ears would be ringing from the comparisons between Michael Jordan of the Bulls and Patrick Ewing of the Knicks on who did what from the last game or who was a better player. The owner, Mr. Marion was also a pastor and prominent member of the community. The noise level was high because there was always music playing, the TV blasting, people talking, and me with my Gameboy in hand. There was a ton of information being disseminated very quickly. I vividly remember loud conversations and arguments about driving directions to go down south on Route 95. Everyone had a shortcut or record time to arrive in North or South Carolina or Atlanta. They all had a new route or a better way to get to a certain place.

Then there was my dose of current events during the OJ Simpson trial. Most of the guys vehemently believed that OJ committed the crime, but they wanted him to get off. At the time, I did not really understand it, but I also had this overwhelming feeling of wanting him to get off. It was the OJ documentary that was poignant and a cornerstone in my memory. Those barbershop visits were a prominent time in my life and I was able to take the debate-like conversations and apply them to my school work. I was able to be more open-minded, yet vigilant and understood where my position on an issue came from. The barbershop shaped my views of the world.

At school, our class watched the Simpson verdict with my teacher Mr. Howard, a Black man. He had pride about the verdict and how Black people in America were finally doing something to white people. We had heated conversations regarding OJ Simpson, Rodney King, and the police killing unarmed people of color. During that time, I recall the Black community feeling lost and frustrated over the recent senseless killings. Although not much has changed, I remember feeling the same way, and never understood why I did not like police officers and did not feel safe.

Back then, the fluidity of how there was idea sharing, sharing of services, and information being exchanged at the barbershop felt natural. There wasn't much outward beefs with one another. I remember a client would come to my cousin Sean for a cut and then that client would go to another barber down the street and come back to Sean when he could. I watched how the community recreated some of the good things and connecting with people. Those are the types of things that I wish would come back.

Being at the barbershop during the Million Man March is also etched in my memory. Most of the guys were looking forward to going. I remember the pride I felt about my culture, and how the media continued to say that something like this was not possible, and was never going to happen. I watched how men galvanized and got food, transportation and made it logistically work for their brothers.

Today, when I go to the barbershop, everyone is on their phones. There is no rite of passage and feeling of community for our young Black and Brown men. There were no arguments and debates about a major current event or sports event. I think this generation is missing that connection. We do not have this passive or covert way of passing down belief systems, values, and morals; like my transition from getting a haircut by parents, then a guy coming to my house, and ultimately going to the barbershop.

There was always a code of respect when women walked into the barbershop. If someone was cursing they stopped and apologized. There was always someone cursing. There was a local drug addict who swept the floors and the barbers gave him money. Just that simple exchange and those connections are missing today.

It's funny, I met my barber a week before my wedding. My friend said, "Lewis, your hairline is crooked!" She told me that her husband was an excellent barber and takes his gift as a heaven-sent, God-ordained piece of work. When she said that, I immediately thought of Dr. King when he said, "where ever you find yourself, make sure you are giving your best of the best to do your job." I decided to give her husband a try. I have never looked back. He talked about his faith, family and society. It is such a therapeutic healing process as he pours so much into my life. He is also a connector for me and he is intentional on building relationships to enhance my future.

Barbers and the barbershop experiences are unmatched when it comes to the heart and belly of the community. Some of the stuff is not verbalized, but it is taught by sitting in the barbershop and talking with the people around you. The Jersey City community at large, not just a Black community and I imagine that my Latino brothers experience the same impact.

Looking back, I am grateful that my cousin Sean wanted to make sure he took care of me. He understood my dad's struggles so he voluntarily stood in the gap. Sean always had a good relationship with my dad. My dad was 50 when he died. Sean thought my dad was the coolest uncle in the world and he respected my mom a great deal. Whatever the case, it felt good to have gained Sean's acceptance as a preteen.

Breaking the Curse

"As a Black man in America, I can relate to the demons, of not feeling good enough."

My dad was the youngest boy of nine kids. His dad, my grandfather, died before I was born. I was told that my grandfather was a hard worker and lived in the projects. My father was probably influenced by his older brothers because they were the ones who were around him growing up. Mom told me that Lewis never talked about his father at all. He only spoke highly of his mother because as the youngest, she loved on him all the time.

Lewis had pacemaker surgery around 2002. Ten years later, there were fluids leaking from the hole the doctors left around the device. He went in to have the holes plugged and was under anesthesia. He never recovered. There are countless young men that I meet that say, "F…. my dad! I don't need him! He was never there for me!" I can't convince them of their dad's intentions or circumstances, but I always encourage them to look at the fact that they are here for a reason, and it's up to them to make a difference and break the generational curse for their own families.

My dad passed away in 2012 at St. Michael's Hospital in Newark, New Jersey. I remember the day before he went in for surgery, he called me and talked about wanting grandchildren. I was on my way to a party. Something told me to relax and talk to him. In our typical conversations, we laughed a lot. I was not a sports fan and he loved the Dolphins. We talked about my wife Myriam and how snooty she is, which always made us crack up. We talked about mommy and how crazy she is. I ended the conversation with, "I love you." He responded, "love you too."

The next day he was gone. I knew that my mother hated him-even in death. At the funeral, she walked up to his casket, scoffed, and then held me as I sat on the front row of the church. At the burial site, my dad's brother's and sisters said, "Let's talk about the good times we had." My mother blurted out, "Pshhh! What good times?" At the end of the day, I will always be team mom, but I told her that I needed to have my own experiences with my dad, as she had her own. I gave myself permission to mourn. After all, it was not her dad, it was mine. I had to stand by my truth. The truth was that he was still my father and I didn't feel for him what she felt for him. I needed to experience that mourning in order to grow.

After his death, I realized that he did the best he could with what he was working with. My mom told me that he had a drug addiction and that she purposely did not want me exposed to that. As a kid, you can never see these things in a person you admire or want attention from. Thanks, mommy for always being "Mama Bear" even when I did not see the danger ahead.

To this day, I feel robbed of my full experience with my dad. I felt that we were on to something great and that he was taken prematurely. When my son AJ was born, he did not see his granddad and I wanted that for him. Spending time with my grandkids is a real goal of mine. Sometimes I have thoughts of dying before reaching my fullest potential. Our last day is not up to us. That's why I go hard with everything and give 110% to whatever I do.

The X Factor:

Understanding the Congruence & Similarity of Properties

I often watch the Showtime Series, *Ray Donovan*. Ray is the male version of Scandal's infamous Olivia Pope. However, instead of a setting on Capitol Hill, *Ray Donovan* is set in Los Angeles' Hollywood elite. What often strikes me about this show is the father-son relationship Ray has with his dad. As a celebrity "fixer" Ray thinks he is better than his dad and despises his criminal behaviors. Ray believes he is helping people, while his dad is doing evil. Every time there were scenes between Ray and his dad on the show, I could not help but think of my relationship with my dad. All of my life I have been trying to move up into an elite circle, while my dad was doing things for the community. I sometimes looked down on him, when I should have been looking up to him for helping others.

I don't care how much you despise your parent. When they die, you feel like you've lost your best friend. I've experienced it personally, and I've witnessed it among my peers. Many of them had said in anger, "He wasn't anybody to me. It's whatever!" But mourning brings several things to light. You might not handle your relationships well. You may want to do something drastic like leave your marriage. You may want to experience a life-change, such as cutting all your hair off. My friends experienced all of these things in spite of their initial feelings of numbness. Grief is inevitable, so it behooves us to build that relationship with our less-than-perfect parent. Anyone who talks to me about my dad always says, "He was a cool guy, really down-to-earth." I'm thankful for the privilege to have known him. I've been through a lot of counseling since his death. I can't help but remember him on his birthday, September 1st. On the first birthday after his death, I felt uneasy and agitated around that time. I didn't make the connection right away. My wife sent me a text on that day which said, "I know that you're going through something because of your father's death." Then it all made sense. Looking back, I am grateful for the adult to adult time that I got to spend with my dad. There were father-son moments that I experienced with him that will last a lifetime.

You + Forgiveness = The Answer

I've read many articles that say there is a fatherless crisis in America. Millions of kids are raised without fathers and in the Black family, the percentages are higher. There is a lot of statistical data that shows the negative effects on children when fathers are absent from the home. These negative effects take a toll on the family unit and society in general. For kids growing up without a father, they are more likely to be in poverty-stricken areas, more likely to have been abused, more likely to have behavioral challenges and end up in jail, more likely to abuse drugs and alcohol, more likely to commit crimes, and more likely to drop out of high school. Unfortunately, to add to the absent Black father crisis, statistics show that Black men incarcerated receive longer jail time for similar crimes committed by Caucasian males.

This past summer I took a group of young men to my Uncle Frank's cookout in Long Island. I rented a car for eight young men. Once we arrived, one of them got into the drivers' side and hit a parked car. I was embarrassed and annoyed at the same time. It was a dumb decision and he was a danger to himself and other people. I could not help but read him the riot act for two hours from Long Island to Jersey City. I told his dad and he agreed that his son should pay for the damage. I started to feel bad for him and he said, "Mr. Spears, I'm sorry, I don't want you to lose connection with me." At the end of the day, it is about mentoring and being there for kids. They yearn for someone to be in their corner. Although his dad in his life, he was willing to get into trouble with his dad and not me.

CHAPTER 2

―――∾∾―――

PATTERNS & ASSOCIATIONS

---

*"You have to learn what you're made up of,
and dig deeper to learn who you are to
discover possible ancestral pitfalls."*

The starting point to understanding patterns and associations in my life lies with my mom, Regina Spears. She was already pregnant with me when she and Lewis Morrison went to the prom. I was born on November 29, 1983, at Jersey City Medical Center. Like most teen parents, my mom and dad split up shortly thereafter. My mother had to drop out of high school but went on to get her G.E.D. She was never one to quit or back down from a challenge and could care less about what my dad Lewis was doing. I was a "Lewis" too, but by *first* name only. I lived in Booker T. Washington Projects on Fremont Street with my mom, great-grandmother, two aunts, Diane and Lorraine, and a little woman who was a family friend. Back then, I was the only male living with seven women in a two bedroom apartment.

When I was born, the projects had been in existence since the 1940s and were intended as affordable housing. My maternal great-grandmother, affectionately called Grum, moved out of a house and into the projects because she could not afford to live anywhere else in the area. After we were there a few years, the government modernized the courtyards by pouring concrete paths along the front so you could no longer drive your car right up to the building. They added a basketball court, a playground, a community center, and green metal benches to make it appear family-friendly. We lived on the second floor in Booker T. Growing up, I heard Grum say a number of times, "You always want to live on the second floor. The third floor's too far up and the first floor's too close [to the ground]."

Since my family structure consisted of many women, I gravitated towards them. Aside from Grum, there was my grandmother Pat, who had been physically abused by my grandfather, Eugene. Both of my grandparents abused alcohol. I've been told that Eugene was a nice guy when he wasn't drinking. Grandpa Eugene was abusive to *all* of the women in the house, including my mom and her two sisters, Diane and Lorraine. He got so out of hand one day that when Grum was visiting he knocked Grum's teeth out! Fighting, cussing, and ongoing verbal and physical abuse was common and everyone involved continued with their day because this was the norm.

The Spears family has rehearsed the story of my grandfather as an abusive whoremunger to the younger generation.

Not so much in a boastful or macho manner, but to shed light on his tragic and disrespectful behavior so that others would not follow in either my grandfather Eugene or grandma Pat's footsteps. I never respected my grandfather because he thought it was so cool to have a lot of women. At the age of nine, I remember asking him, "Who is your wife?" He would say, "I don't have a wife, I have this woman and that woman. That's what I do!"

When I was 12, I got into an altercation with my cousin and my grandfather grabbed me and pulled me off of him. I cursed my grandfather and he smacked me. It was messy. I had no respect for him after that, nor did I trust him. Grandpa Eugene finally picked up and moved on, yet he ended up with another "Pat," who gave birth to my mom's half-sister, Sheranda.

Despite its dysfunction, the Spears family was always tight. My aunts were like an extension of my mother. If Mommy wasn't around, I got handled by them. Our house was constantly filled with cigarette smoke and alcohol. It's mind-boggling when I think about the health hazards of the second-hand smoke my siblings and I were exposed to for so many years. Nobody knew about the dangers back then. The adults were doing what they could to survive and during that time, it was nothing short of tumultuous, day in and day out. Fights broke out over kids messing something up, owing someone money as little as five dollars, a rude comment, or having sex with someone else's girlfriend or boyfriend.

My great-grandma Grum, always kept a case of short Budweiser cans in the fridge that she sold for a dollar after the liquor store closed at 9 PM. Can you imagine the random people coming through our house all hours of the night to grab a beer? My mom and aunts were always getting into arguments with Grum over copping a beer without paying for it. All of this commotion was going on despite the fact that I had to go to school in the morning; I don't think I slept soundly for many years.

My Grandma Pat died of cirrhosis of the liver when I was four. This was around the same time my mother was giving birth to my brother Kayvon at Jersey City Medical Center. Kayvon had eczema and he did not come home right away. I remember him having a grayish skin color when he came home. Mom was so excited that I now had a baby brother.

Alcohol abuse has been a prevalent generational curse in the Spears family. Men abusing women has also been par for the course. These destructive cyclical issues are deeply rooted. I decided that it was my responsibility to take charge and break the curse. To start, I began implementing family meetings where I have called out individual's negative behaviors and their good ones. I am intentional about how I deal with my family. I call my mom, stepdad, siblings, aunts, and cousins to tell them I love them and to remind them of who they are and the value that they have in my life. I make sure to suggest counseling for any issues that are challenging to them. I am not ashamed to discuss the benefits counseling has had on my life. I butt heads and get frustrated with family members often because I know that you can lead a horse to water but you can't make him drink. Some things stick and some don't, but I will not give up trying to help.

My mother helped raise *all* of the kids in the family, including her sisters and their children. My oldest female cousin is two years older than me and my younger female cousins are two to four years under me. Mommy got up with them for their morning routines to get them off to school. Whatever she did for me, she did for them also. Mommy was a homebody. My aunts hung out all the time and were known to "rip and run the streets" as the elders said back then. Mom stayed in the house and was very domestic. She was the one who knew how to cook and just take care of business. Mommy was like the project's *Dr. Quinn, Medicine Woman*, and everyone called on her for home remedies. Bottom line, Mommy was the most responsible person in my family. Yet underneath her tough exterior, she still felt like she wasn't good enough.

It hurts to see the women in my family lose all hope, with no goals and dreams over a no-good guy. We have vision board parties to get them to see themselves differently. We discuss their purpose and my wife and I do everything we can to help them identify goals for the future. Whether my family or yours, we need to take an active role in uplifting and empowering one another as often as we can. I've learned, that if you want to make a change and turn negative statistics in your hood to positive, it starts at home, with your family.

> *"If you lie to yourself about your own pain, you will be killed by those who will claim you enjoyed it."*
> — **Alice Walker, Possessing the Secret of Joy**

Mommy was molested by her cousin Alvin between the ages of 5-10. Alvin was also her godfather. My mother's history of sexual abuse made her extra protective of me and my siblings. She'd say things like, "We're not getting close to people because that's what they'll do to you! If anyone ever tried to touch you, I would kill them!" I straight up believed her. My mother was 'bout it" and couldn't care less about the consequences. The ironic thing was that my stepfather, Kenny, closely resembled her cousin Alvin.

I remember one day when Mommy cried out to Grum. That incident always stuck out to me because my mother was *not* a crier. She told Grum that my grandmother Pat never loved her. My mom had a hard time being the middle child. She believed that her sister Diane was loved more by their father and that her sister Lorraine was loved by both their mother and grandmother. In her mind, it seemed valid, especially given all the attention they placed on Lorraine and helped support her.

I don't recall Mommy throwing the molestation in Grandma Pat's face, but she was always saying something like, "You doin' them better than me!" Grandma responded, "You're good. You don't need any help." My mother shot back, "I don't want to hear that bull!" Grandma Pat told her that she did not focus on her and us kids because she felt my mom was good. My mom was responsible and could take care of herself. That was never enough for my mom. She wanted my grandmother to love her a certain way. In hindsight, I don't think Grandma Pat had an ounce left to give. She had been physically and verbally abused by men for so long, that she eased her pain and anger with alcohol, until her death.

My mom and Kenny tied the knot in 1992 and everyone in the house's name changed to "White." Mom was now Regina White, my brother Kayvon White, and my sister Kamiesha White. I was the only "Spears" in the house. Psychologically, I stood out. It did something to me. Wow! *I was really the odd man out.* I thought. It was us a family unit, then in marriage, I became a separate, sole entity. I felt that they were a family and I was not. Mom thought it was no big deal with the name thing, "what you complaining about? Spears is a good name!" In hindsight, I'm glad that I get to carry the Spears name and break the negative cycle and generational curse of men in the family mistreating the women in the family. I talked with my mom about being molested by her cousin a few years ago and she never realized how much Kenny and Alvin looked alike. Yet, when I thought more about it, since mom's cousin Alvin was her first encounter with a man, even though she was a child, he became how she viewed men in the world.

GRUM THE GREAT

My great-grandmother, Grum was a school bus attendant. She was only 4'11" and very petite, but she went about her business like a person of strong and almost royal stature. She had long silver hair that my cousin Tamika was required to brush and braid into different styles. Grum wore long or short sleeve sweaters and jeans with the permanent crease in them, which were the perfect length. She enjoyed her job and took it seriously, although she made very little money. I was always interested in storytelling and she would tell me stories about my dad. Most of the time they were funny or gave me insight into his character.

As a child, I knew that when I walked through Grum's threshold everything was going to be good and safe. I felt so much love. Even though she was not the kind of grandma that kissed on you, you knew that she had your back no matter what. Grum's house was spotless and always smelled like Pine Sol, if she wasn't cooking. There was clear plastic with pointed edges covering her brown and beige couch, loveseat and chair. Her furniture had geometric patterns and shapes. There were also plastic runners on the floor, and if you walked too quickly, and your foot accidentally turned up one corner, your foot stuck to the runner like suction cups.

Grum was the smartest person I knew. She watched *Jeopardy* while doing crossword puzzles and was very good at both. She was also an amazing cook and made chitterlings on New Year's for good luck and other family staples during the holidays. I still despise the pungent smell of chitterlings, and could never bring myself to even taste a small bite. To this day, no one in the family or otherwise comes close to her mac and cheese and beef stew recipes - no one. Grum was also very organized and always had her Sunday dinner cooked by 10 AM. She was consistent with her Sunday music playing in the background. Whenever I think of her, I hear the song, "I'm coming up on the rough side of the mountain," by Rev. FC Barnes & Company. It was definitely her favorite and it became mine as well.

I enjoyed hearing grown-up conversations even if I did not know exactly what was going on. I hid under Grum's dining room table to get the 411 on family gossip. Every time I heard my mother cursing her grandmother, I was uncomfortable because my Grum was so even-keeled, kind and spiritual. She let mommy rant and rave without interjecting. I guess she felt sorry for my mom and knew that mom needed to get out her anger about life's disappointments off her chest. I wanted to stand up for my great-grandmother, but since I was taught to stay out of grown folks business, I didn't say a word. My mom probably would have slapped me upside my head anyway.

I knew my great-grandmother Grum trusted me because she started sending me to A & S Grocery Store downtown when I was only 10 years old. Unlike my other cousins, she knew that I would bring back the right amount of change. One day, she sent me to get milk and there was another young man who was sent to get milk by his family also. He spent his money on something that he shouldn't have and started coming for my milk. We were tussling back and forth, and my old Nike sneakers were screeching on the grocery store floor. "Yo, I have to get home with this milk!" I yelled. *I wasn't having it - not today* was my immediate thought. "Yo, give me the milk," he said through clenched teeth as he punched me square in the face. I dropped the milk, ran after him, and punched him in the back. He kept running.

I went back to the store and picked up my family's milk. As small as it may seem, fighting to bring milk home had a big impact on my life and represented something so much greater on the inside. It was my understanding of responsibility. I now had a responsibility to make sure the people in my house were taken care of. I doubt if Grum would've responded negatively if I didn't deliver, but I knew she was depending on me, so I had to come through at any cost. Even if it meant a swollen face.

Grum died when I was 12 years old. I still feel the void today. I spent the most time with Grum on a regular basis. I learned how to cook, clean, and fix things around the house. I learned about relationships with people and having a connection to God. I sat and talked with her and listened to her spiritual music which I believe gave me confidence. I had this sense of strength and courage to lead the family by doing the right thing at *all* times. Everything Grum said to me was golden. On her deathbed, she told my mother and other family members to watch me because I was going to be something good. I instantly felt like I became the patriarch of the family at 12 years old. Every decision I made, I did it with the intent on pleasing Grum. When I'm stressed, I think about how Grum would handle the situation. I still wonder what life would be like if Grum were alive.

Earning My Keep

My family was subject to the social staples of the hood which meant Section 8, welfare, W.I.C., and food stamps were an integral part of our lives. I went to the store on school days with food stamps to buy penny candy. I used a one dollar food stamp to buy five pieces of candy and would get .95 cents cash back. I needed the change to pay for lunch so my friends would not know that I had food stamps. The great thing about my hood was that you did not have to go far for whatever you wanted. I went to Sluggo's on the corner of Jackson and Bostwick Avenue for the best turkey and cheese sandwiches around. Sluggos also had a laundromat. Then there was Mumbles downtown in Lafayette Projects in the basement that smelled like a combination of smoke and a stale, wet concrete basement. My cousins and I played ping-pong, bought penny candy, Slim Jim's and slices of Pizza for $1.25 from Mumbles. There was also a mini arcade with

PacMan, Streetfighter and pool tables. People shot pool all hours of the night and just hung out to smoke and drink in the atmosphere. Everyone knew each other and felt safe because someone always had your back. I didn't get to stay out too late because after 9:00 PM, all of the adults in my family hung out at "Pete's" bar across the street from Booker T., while I babysat my siblings and cousins.

Extended Family

Living in Booker T. Projects was like going on an adventure. You had to be mentally prepared for the day's challenges. At times, I became my own superhero in my mind. If I didn't, I would be eaten alive. Not literally of course, but I would be bullied, threatened or jumped at any given moment for any whim or transgression that my challenger could think of. I was very observant, cautious, and tried to outsmart the troublemakers. Yet I felt safe in my hood. It was a community within a community, with insider rules to abide by. Outsiders were not welcome.

There was nonstop activity. I know they say that New York City is the city that never sleeps, well in my hood in Jersey City, there were a lot of sheisty things happening 24/7: drug deals, robberies, shooting dice, fights, killings and other corruption. As kids, we knew we couldn't step into the hallway when certain drug dealers or a stick-up kid were present. We were always on high alert to make sure we were nowhere around because you were guaranteed to get robbed, beat down or caught in the middle of a drug deal gone bad.

It was common to get into a fight for winning a basketball game if your opponent was feeling dissed. On the other hand, you could borrow ketchup or sugar from your neighbors every week, just like family. There were organized bus trips in the summer to Dorney Park, Six Flags, Washington D.C., and other family-friendly places both in and outside of New Jersey. Since we were considered poor, we paid little or no money for these excursions as many of them were funded by a government program.

During the day, in the summertime, it was family versus family in kickball, baseball and football in the courtyard. There were volleyball and basketball tournaments that everyone stuck around to watch. It was intense. Sometimes the matches escalated into projects versus projects, which was something everyone definitely looked forward to. There was food, drinks, and music playing all summer long. In the winter, we were limited to football in the snow.

Early on, I lived on the hill of Booker T and Lafayette Projects was across the street. Booker T was a different hood than on the hill. I had to adapt to different environments. It was as if every few blocks had their own set of rules. Crime, corruption, and destruction were becoming the norm. I remember the owner of Sluggos had speakers on top of his car driving down the streets reading the Bible and praying for the community. That image of him driving down Jackson Avenue (now MLK), will always be a vivid memory. I believe that Grum's prayers and the Sluggo's prayers worked for me. I would stop dead in my tracks while the car drove by. Some words of Scripture resonated as if he was talking directly to me, "*God loves you no matter what you have done. Seek God. He hears you and will answer your prayers.*" I always felt a sense of spirituality on the inside, that soft inner voice guiding me to keep me out of trouble and show me things from a different perspective. That inner voice and revelations were always stronger when I was in the presence of Grum. Back then, my community needed prayer, and it needs even more prayer today. I believe everyone and every city could use more prayer.

One of my favorite memories growing up in Jersey City was when Mommy took us downtown to play with our cousins. We played tag, hopscotch, hide-and-go-seek, or just ran around aimlessly. Grum cooked on the regular and we all had our favorite dishes like cornbread and salmon cakes which were off the chain. Going downtown was a treat and there were times when Grum sent me downtown on my own. One of the best spots downtown was A&S Grocery Store (the one where that dude tried to jack my milk) which was a tri-part store: liquor, food, and pizzeria. They also had a check-cashing spot.

The barometer for success in the hood was just mere comparison. Everyone judged each other's hang ups. Aunt Diane would say, "At least I drink. All my other friends are getting high!" Somehow, being an alcoholic made her better than drug users. My mom's go to line was, "At least I got married and moved out of the projects. I got *two* cars!" The common thread amongst these women was that they still possessed a poverty mindset and drank every weekend.

The Red Corner

My real father, Lewis, didn't know that my mom was getting beat by her husband Kenny. She even tried to hide it from the family. I was disgusted by the fact that she was so strong but so weak at the same time. Everyone in the Spears family knew what was going on. Aunt Diane was in a relationship with Kenny's brother, better known as "Speed" and she was getting beat regularly. Aunt Lorraine was being beaten by her man also, so the three sisters had come to the point where they shared stories of their abuse. I was told that Grandma Pat couldn't stand Kenny or Speed because she did not think either of them was not good enough for her daughters. She considered them low lives and abusers who got their thrills putting their hands on females. Kenny reminded Pat of her ex, my grandpa Eugene, so she did not want mom or her daughters to go through what she went through.

Mommy and Kenny started fighting a lot when I was around eight years old. I remember me and Kayvon were standing in a corner crying when Kenny was getting the best of her. Kenny was on top of her and threw punches. We never knew from day-to-day what was going to be an argument or what was going to trigger all-out blows. I had to manage both my parents and my siblings. I had to stay two steps ahead of

Mommy and Kenny by making provisions to take care of my brother and sister. *My mind was always in this think quickly mode: They might argue tonight, so let me get Kayvon and Kamiesha situated, make sure they're sleepin' in bed. Let me get them out of harm's way if they're gonna throw down.* It wasn't every night, but we knew one wrong word from Mommy could lead to a slap in the mouth or a push. It was consistently dysfunctional and unstable.

Mommy's motto became: "Whatever happens in my house stays in my house. I don't want you tellin' my business to nobody!" The three of us kids always nodded in agreement. So whenever they fought we kept it to ourselves. Aunt Diane liked to question us in a certain way to get what she wanted to know from us. She never came out and asked, did he hit her? Instead, she'd say, "so how are things going?" We knew she meant it, so we responded with a nonchalant, "fine." The mere thought of mommy's business getting out would mean all hell would break loose!

I remember one day when I was about 10 years old, there were at least eight or nine of us riding in Kenny's 1987 yellow Cadillac DeVille with tan leather seats. The glue that held the cloth to the roof had worn out so we all had a hand in holding the roof up while Kenny drove. I enjoyed being a wise-mouth, especially when it came to Kenny and I said, "I don't know why we are all in here, Kenny don't have a license!" Mommy gave me that look. Later that day she tore me up! After every blow, she said, "Who told you to open your big mouth! They don't know Kenny don't have a license! Don't you ever talk about nothing that happened in my household. Ever!" Again, I know I said it because I just couldn't stand him at the time, but I really loved that car. It was the first car I attempted to drive.

Although there were celebratory moments we had as a family, the three of us kids were constantly in fear as we anticipated an argument. Even though we went out to dinner at Sizzlers and had Sunday dinner at Grum's or aunt Lorraine's house, a fight could break out between Mommy and Kenny the moment we got home.

One night, Kenny was getting the best of my mother and I felt helpless. A few days later, we were at my aunt Diane's and mommy witnessed Kenny's brother Speed curse him out. Kenny didn't say a word. That's when mommy got the courage to fight back.

BOOM!! "Oh, you can beat your woman but you can't stand up to your brother?" "I knew you were a punk," she chided. That's how Mommy found her strength and I admire her for it. To this day, after every phone conversation, before hanging up she says, "Lewis, don't take no wooden nickels." Thanks, Mommy.

After that, I started speaking out as well. I reminded Kenny all the time, "You ain't my father!" Mommy clearly loved me more than him and he knew he couldn't compete with me. Looking back, I was great in school, but a terror as a step-kid. Kenny was my target and I was super critical of him. I sided with Mommy because she was the one who took care of me. I saw her stress and hurt daily. I remember coming home after a hard day at school and giving Kenny the cold shoulder. He sensed my attitude and asked, "Whas wrong wit chu?" I kept ignoring him so he jumped up to hit me, but Mommy got in between us. I fell to the floor. Mommy laid on top of me and Kenny was on top of her, struggling to get to me. We just couldn't see eye to eye. I wasn't his and he made that clear. I'll never forget the time he punched me repeatedly while he was screaming, "Stop being gay!" I didn't understand any of it then, and he apologized years later, but it still hurt.

"They
say you took my manhood,
Momma.
Come sit on my lap
and tell me,
what do you want me to say
to them, just
before I annihilate
their ignorance ?"
Son to Mother, Maya Angelou

The Strength of a Woman

... I will survive

My mom is amazing. She was always tough, but I knew that she loved me. Unfortunately, my stepdad knew that too.

Around fourth grade, Mommy was home during the day and worked from 3:00-11:00 PM. She always worked more than one job and back then she started working at a daycare center and I was able to go to daycare with her to hang out while she watched the kids. Despite her toughness, she was very nurturing and attentive to our needs. Dinner was on the table every night. On the rare occasion that I actually had to cook for Kayvon and Kamiesha, it would be an Oodles of Noodles night. I was responsible for making sure my brother and sister did their homework. My stepdad, Kenny, mainly slept and went to work. On weekends, he went out to chill with his friends or to his mother's house.

I considered Mommy to be a single parent because Kenny wasn't my father, and we were with her 95% of the time. It was rare for Kenny to do something with us as a family unit. Mommy went grocery shopping on her own. She did laundry, folded the clothes and put them away. Kenny never lifted a finger around the house. If he cooked, it was only on Saturday mornings, because he was hungry and mommy announced that she wasn't cooking. He'd offer us leftovers with a generous, "Ya'll could eat!" Of the three of us, Kayvon was the only one who Kenny clung to. Even though Kenny had a son before marrying my mother, his son's mother did not allow Kenny to see him. It was as if Kayvon was his first son. I believe Kenny also clung to my brother because Kayvon knew how to keep a secret. Kenny was cheating on Mommy and Kayon kept it on the hush for years. Even my aunts caught Kenny shopping in a supermarket with another female. My brother often alluded to the fact that Kenny was no saint, but he never came out and gave details. It was clear that they shared a secret.

Mommy held a lot of resentment towards Kenny for his actions and inaction. Her emotions were never intact and she could go off in a second. She had her own set of character flaws and she drank E & J Dark Liquor which she called "Easy Jesus" and was never short on Budweiser. On top of the drinking, she smoked Newport 100's daily, just to cope. She was "Mama Bear" and proud of it, and she became very domineering towards Kenny. She reminded Kenny on a regular basis, "I don't need you, you piece of crap!" Mommy emasculated and berated Kenny to no end. She'd say to him, "Shut the hell up! These are *my* kids. You don't know what you're doing. You can't do nothing for me. You don't know how to satisfy me."

Another 360 Degree Turnaround

It wasn't until I got older that I learned that Kenny is Geechie. There was a level of embarrassment on his part. There is a culture and rich history of the Geechie people in the South, and why their language is necessary for survival. Everything from the food they eat to the spiritual rituals gave me a new-found appreciation for him. Kenny lives in Jersey City a few minutes from where I work. He actually helps out Kayvon's children and their mother as they all live together. Kenny has changed so much in terms of his commitment to the family.

He has played the role of dad and now grandpa, and calls my wife and me often to check in on our son AJ, who loves his grits and potato salad. Kenny is adamant about making sure that he has those foods for AJ when AJ visits. I am forever grateful to see Kenny's turnaround.

Like my dad Lewis, I believe Kenny did not know how to be a man. Deep inside, I felt that Kayvon's birth changed our relationship. Kenny and I were close until Kayvon was born. Then our relationship deteriorated. Kenny was mean to me and unfair at times. We went to Kenny's family reunion a few years ago and he told us how no one taught him how to be a man, so he had to teach himself. He turned 60 and now realizes that it is not too late to start. Kenny is very transparent and gives me pointers on how to treat my wife. Our relationship has evolved a full 360 degrees.

Now that I am older, I feel a sense of ownership to say that he is connected to me, a real part of my family. I never felt like that before. For years, I would say to others, "he's my mother's husband, or he's my sister's dad." I am proud to call him stepdad and pop. I was recently talking to my mom about AJ going to a babysitter. She said, "Call Kenny, he will keep him." Like I said, call Kenny." Kenny was a horrible husband, but a good father to all of his children. My son AJ calls him pop-pop. As a man, I understand the dynamics of what was going on back then. Yet there's one thing I know for sure, I wouldn't be able to take the verbal abuse that my mom dished out to Kenny if my wife spoke to me that way.

41

Thinking about it now, and especially writing it down is definitely cringe-worthy. In those days I didn't even wince because it seemed normal. My brother, sister and I just sat there thinking, *here we go again*. Mommy continued mouthing off even though it sometimes got her punched in the face. I believe she was just mad enough to pick a fight with Kenny because she wasn't afraid of anyone. She fought boys growing up, so jumping in Kenny's mug wasn't anything new.

The truth of the matter is that I had never heard of Mommy having a fight with a female. She proudly proclaimed, "That's because after they saw what I did to their brothers, they didn't want to mess with me!" Anyone who knew Mommy always said, "Don't play with your mother!" She got away with saying crazy stuff to other women but they didn't try her. They let her say whatever she pleased and surrendered with "Regina crazy!" She was like a bear. She would tear your head off if you came at her sideways. No one could "come out their face" to me, Kayvon or Kamiesha; whether man, woman, old person or a cripple. I was told by family members when I was just two years old, my great aunt asked, "Whas wrong with that boy? Is he retarded?" Mommy went off on her and never spoke to her again.

The PJ's Hustle

People in the projects were making money and being creative geniuses. I remember there was a store in a person's house. Since people were up 24/7, when the local stores closed, you could go to Mrs. Joyce's house in Apartment 3B in Booker T. She had penny candy, Twizzlers, Laffy Taffy's, Peanut Chews and Boston Baked Beans. She also sold sandwiches and other pre-made food, CDs, radios, walkmans, and even portable TV's! Of course, most if not all, of the electronic merchandise was stolen. Yet it was like a badge of honor that you had to take care of your family by any means necessary.

Everybody had a card game hustle. This meant that they hosted card games in their apartment which included Pitty-Pat. Spades, and 7-Card Poker. There was a card club of 10-15 people who went to each other's houses weekly. It was almost like a sou-sou, but they weren't pooling all their money together, yet everyone had a chance to collect a certain amount of money based upon their play strategy and luck.

The funny thing is that it was everyone's normal. It's how Mommy met Kenny during a card game. He was in a relationship with another woman, who had his 3-month old daughter. Mommy was friendly with this woman, but she stole Kenny from her. Years later, Mommy and this woman all wound up playing on the same card circuit again. Kenny would come home after work and they'd both be there, playing cards. It was convoluted, but this woman never tried to fight my mom. I guess it was because Mommy already had a reputation for being a fighter or she knew that Kenny was no good and not worth fighting for.

Whoever hosted the game circle fed the guests spaghetti, fried chicken, potato salad and greens, liquor and the best

R&B music. If you did not have food or liquor, no one would play at your party. The catch was to make it as comfortable as possible. The table was usually a $25 table stake. Only six people could play per table and it was $5 per hand. The winner received $25 because $5 went to the house. So the more food and booze you had with two tables going, the more you could make as the host. People started playing as soon as they got home from work and they left at 6 AM the next morning. Players were allowed to borrow money from the house. It was really crazy.

During the card games, younger kids were encouraged to go outside or stay in the back room. When I was old enough, I was the server to the guests in a room full of cigarette smoke. I made plates and handed out sodas and beer. The great thing about being a server was that I got a cut at the end of the night. This allowed the host to focus on tables and the money. I started playing with the adults when I was around 16. Before then, my cousins and I would be in the room playing for money. The seed was planted for my competitiveness and gambling itch.

In high school, I spent about $10 a day playing cards. We played Pitty Pat in English class under the desk. I was gambling every day with my friends. I had it bad when I was a teenager and young adult. My grandfather and uncles did not like playing with me because if I won, I would get up and leave the table and never gave them a chance to win their money back.

Another common hustle in the PJ's was hairdressers. My mom did not have long hair. She wore a low thick fro that was unmanageable. Mom never over-processed her hair, and she had a complex about her short hair at times, but then she would say things like, "Oh well it's me!" She never went to the beauty parlor to get her hair done. Instead, she went downstairs in our building so Niecey could put in her Jheri curl. She was adamant about Niecey's skills. If someone even fixed their mouth to recommend another hairdresser, Mommy was quick to say, "Oh no, Niecey's the only one who can touch my hair, cuz she the one who made my hair grow!"

The X Factor: Patterns & Associations

"Nobody wins when the family feuds
We all screwed 'cause we never had the tools
I'm tryna fix you...
Y'all think small, I think Biggie
Y'all whole pass is in danger, ten Mississippi
Al Sharpton in the mirror takin' selfies
How is him or Pill Cosby 'posed to help me?...
We all lose when the family feuds
What's better than one billionaire? Two..."
Jay Z, Family Feud

I think it is important to know various characteristics and traits of immediate family members to direct you down a path to make better choices than they did. The Spears family DNA has years of domestic violence, and alcohol abuse. A large part of it stems from poverty, lack of education and negative views of self-worth. I have to be mindful that I am the product of both Lewis and Regina and some of their insecurities and shortcomings try to rear their head in my life. I am on high alert to eliminate them as soon as possible. My mom still has moments of doubt and not being good enough like when she was younger crying out to her mother and grandmother for love and attention. She never got the unconditional love she needed from her parents to give her the confidence grow.

Mommy still makes comparisons to me about how I treat my aunt, who is also my godmother. If I take my aunt out for lunch or dinner, she complains about how often I take her out. Or she will bring up a time when I took AJ to visit my aunt and did not stop by her house. Oftentimes, I just don't know what to say. I would never intentionally hurt my mother. I have taken care of her emotionally my entire life, to the point where I am overly conscious, or walking on eggshells to make sure she is good.

She can also be tempermental about the things you say, how you look at her or what you do for her. Her outbursts cause conflicts with other family members. To keep the peace, I run and jump at her request. I can't help but react the same way to my mom that I do to my wife and even my friends. I am constantly running around putting out fires to help others. I have to be intentional to love on my wife and show her gratitude in spite of what I am doing for others.

You + Recognizing Familial Patterns = the Answer

A key aspect of my growth in therapy was acknowledging and accepting the cards that have been dealt to me as it relates to my DNA. I had a front row seat to the impact of drugs, alcohol, sexual abuse, and violence. That exposure clearly demonstrated that if I chose that path, I would be headed down an unproductive life of destruction. I made the decision very early on that I just wanted more for myself. Change really starts with a decision. So if you are cutting school, hanging with the trouble-making homeboys, and engaging in criminal activity, because that's what everyone in your family does, then it's time to change. It's time to start with a clean slate before you get too deep in the negativity that it takes years to get out. You don't have to be like everyone else. Who knows, maybe your purpose here was to help your family do more and be more.

More important, I believe a lack of education can really keep people in bondage. Whether it's my hood or your hood, there is another way of life a few miles away. Exposure to new environments, ways of doing things, and handling relationships can be a lifeline. Education is not just book knowledge and getting a degree, it is learning from those who are doing something positive that you aspire to do as well. Find a mentor. Find your group who have also made the decision to do better. Hold each other accountable. Even though you may look like your father, your brother, or your uncle, you are not them. Yes, you all share the same DNA, but each one of you has a specific purpose on Earth. Stop playing games and find yours.

CHAPTER 3

---∿---

ME & THE NUMBER SYSTEM
Rationality

If you think you are beaten, you are;
If you think you dare not, you don't;
If you'd like to win, but think you can't,
It's almost a cinch you won't.
If you think you'll lose, you're lost,
For out in the word we find
Success begins with a fellow's will,
It's all in the state of mind.
If you think you're outcasted, you are;
You've got to think high to rise.
You've got to be sure of yourself before
You can ever win a prize.
Life's battles don't always go
To the stronger or faster man;
But soon or late the man who wins
Is the man who thinks he can.
*Thinking, by **Walter D. Wintle***

This poem is by far one of my favorite reminders over the years that I can achieve anything as long as I have the right mindset. Whatever you think in your heart, that is truly who are.[1] *Thinking* illustrates that our mindset determines our success or failure in life. I've always been critical of myself to the point where I became my worst enemy. Yet in spite of all of my sometimes futile outlook of my future, deep down inside, I had a strong desire to succeed and go farther than anyone in my family or in my hood ever imagined possible.

Now that I am older, I often think about my grandfather Eugene. Although I did not admire him when I was younger because he did a lot of negative things to the women in my family, he did one positive thing for me. Grandpa Eugene was the one who eventually got us all together to go to church. I wanted my church experience to be authentic and make it solely mine so I got baptised when I was 10 years old, in the 5th grade. Mommy did not make it to the baptism, but she was very proud that I did it.

I had to wear all white and I remember going down in the water and coming up and not feeling any differently. I thought it did not work! Afterward, I had a conversation with Mrs. Davis, the church bus driver on the way home. She told me that God was in my heart and my decision to get baptised and accept him was all I needed. "Boy, it worked! You'll see," was how she ended it. I connected with the church and was

---

1 Proverbs 23:7

picked up in a van every Sunday. To this day, I believe it was my spiritual connection to God that made me feel special and different, and also kept me from being a total knucklehead.

I was very non-confrontational as a kid. I just wanted to get along with everybody. I remember I had a fight with my best friend Mike. He was a few months older than me, so I didn't think I could beat him. We got into it outside in the dirt and he started wailing on me. Deep down I didn't want to fight him, because he was my friend. With the blows he was landing, I figured I was gonna lose anyway. Then I heard my mother shout out the window, "Lewis, you better hit him back!" She was like a bulldozer-an unstoppable force. I think Mike let me get in a hit or two so as to not let my mother down. By the end of the day, Mike and I were chillin' at his house, eating Rap Snacks, you know the ones with Lil Romeo on the bag. I was a snack king. I used to mix pretzels and sour cream and onion potato chips in a bag and shake them up. I ate honey buns with the block of government American cheese.

I wasn't a goody-two-shoes all the time. There were things that occurred in my life that made me realize what I should and should not have been doing. My boys and I got the bright idea to steal from the corner store. I was the only one who got caught and the store owner made sure I knew that would be my last time trying something like that and he went upside my head. We came out of the store and my friends were hysterical like, "Yo, you wildin Lewis!" Meanwhile, they're pulling out the cupcakes and devil dogs they had stolen. It was cool that they were generous enough to share with me.

Looking back, I only had three fights my entire life. In the hood, that is like a few hours in one day. The first was the guy who tried to steal my milk, then Mike, and then a guy who stole my bike. I never hit that guy back. He was about 16 and I was 12. My cousin was with me. The guy said, "Give me your bike!" I said, "No!" He punched me in the face and I gave up the bike and went home crying.

My cousin Tammia, on my father's side let me know that she cared about me. "Stop crying!" she shouted. She then walked me up and down two or three blocks to find him. I'm glad she did not find him because she would have done something crazy to him. It was the first time someone on my father's side made me feel rescued. She told me to go home and it would be OK. She was the cousin that wore red fingernail polish and offered herself to men for a few dollars to get her next fix. To this day, I get an attitude when I see women wear red polish. Visuals and memories of cousin Tammia crowd my mind.

I still see my old friend Mike when I go back to my hood. Mike and I had a different value system. His grandmom sent him to a private school. I went to public school and did well. He spent most of his time outside playing ball, smoking weed and getting girls. I was more into going to school and sitting home reading. We eventually grew apart. His mom had conversations with me about continuing to be his friend as she appreciated our connection. Mike always had a good heart, yet he never seemed to make good decisions. Even now when I see him it is all love. Mike had a baby recently, so we now have fatherhood in common.

Every time I go back to my hood I can almost picture my boys and I playing the dozens by the court. We cracked on each other all day. None of us had anything, but I guess we were cracking on whoever had nothing the most. When it was all said and done, each of us went home broke. Since we all had roaches, we cracked on whoever had the most roaches and tried to justify it. "At least I only got roaches in my kitchen - you got roaches everywhere!" Then we talked about whoever's parent was a crackhead. It's pretty startling to think about it now, but there were so many good parents who became crackheads. We knew who the "dirty ones" were even though we *all* lived in the projects. We talked about those in the crew whose sneakers were leaning to the side from being worn out. We snapped on the girls with the pigtails and the guys who could not play ball. Whatever your shortcoming or deficiency was, it was definitely up for grabs. I had no problem playing you out. I paid attention to people and always had three negative things to say about them if they ever came for me. I was always ready. It was all cool and jovial. At the end of the day, no one was taking shorts.

We played the nasty games like "7 Minutes in Heaven." Girls would run and guys chased them. If a girl was caught you would have to kiss her for seven minutes or do anything that the guy asked. I had kissed a few girls but not for seven minutes. I heard stories of other guys doing sexual things for seven minutes. We also played "Catch a Girl, Get a Girl," which was the same idea and you had to kiss the girl and then rap to her. Some guys took it literally. I hung out with my cousins and ran up and down the street, mostly running my mouth. I also played "Sonic the Hedgehog" with them in the house for hours. If we were outside, we played "Ace, Queen, King, Jack" on the basketball court.

I could not believe it when this girl named April, from around the way, took a liking to me. She was six years older than me. April was short, light-skinned with huge breasts. In my eyes she was average. My aunt was dating her brother. I'd walk April to the store around the corner from my house on Bergen Ave. I felt souped when she told people, "Thas my little boyfriend." On one of our walks she casually said, "Lewis, I'm hearing rumors from the other guys that you're not one of the guys." "What chu mean?" I asked with raised eyebrows. "I don't see you in the street with the guys or playing football or talking about sex. I don't see you touchin' no girls' butts." I was completely shocked. "You still my boyfriend though," she said as she looked away, trying not to make me any more uncomfortable than I already was. Peer pressure is a terrible thing. Actually, any type of pressure can be stressful. I had nothing to prove.

I was content having conversations with adults, which is why I didn't try to keep up with the other guys who were

13 and 14 years old. I really didn't care about being around teenagers. I always liked to do my own thing. However, after April's comment, I started trying to do "guy things" like playing and watching football. That's when my quest for "What does it mean to be a guy?" began. Prior to that, it all seemed like "regular stuff." I didn't realize that there was "guy stuff" and "girl stuff."

Stir Up the Gift

The only time I gravitated towards history was in the 6th grade in 1994 when Nelson Mandela became President of South Africa. We all had such a precursor to a lot of other things we were learning. My homeroom teacher Mr. Howard, was not only a history teacher but a great mentor. He was instrumental in educating my peers and me on apartheid and the Civil Rights Movement. We were fortunate to have Mr. Howard for three years in a row because the educational system implemented a program called looping which allowed a group of kids to stay with the same teacher in an effort to achieve growth in learning.

I really wanted to learn more about South Africa and how they were able to get away with apartheid for so long. It impacted me strongly as my teacher had a visceral reaction to it. It was such a genuine and intense emotion when we found out that Nelson Mandela won the presidency. The yearning to go to Africa was always there and I was blessed to travel to South Africa in graduate school and even visited Soweto where Mandela lived. It was a breathtaking, hairraising moment. I walked into the house that he lived in, the one where they were shooting at when he went to the jail the first time. It was so amazingly awesome!

We were also learning about the struggle with Brother Rahman. He was a clean brother, with flawless skin and he did not eat meat. I never met a person who didn't eat meat! It was crazy. We looked up to him and were part of a math and science program in Newark, New Jersey.

I was fortunate to have teachers who loved their job of helping their students achieve greater outcomes. My teachers made up the difference in whatever I lacked. Any instruction they provided, I followed it to the letter. So when I was successful, they felt successful. There were 250 kids in my high school class. I graduated number 52. I was in the best program the school had to offer and was generally an A or B student. There were occasional C's, but that was grace because I knew that I was not putting forth any real effort.

In terms of retention and applying certain things in my life, I struggled in that area. I was never good in Language Arts and history - anything that had to do with writing. I tried to take the easy way out more times than not. If I knew the teacher was difficult or the syllabus was hard, I chose another class. Focusing on numbers was the only thing that really excited me and kept me engaged. Geometry, Trigonometry, and Calculus, all still give me an adrenaline rush. I was very active in extracurricular activities and was President of the Student

Council. Yet despite being busy and doing well in my math classes, there were still doubts and lots of uncertainty about my future. I always looked at my shortcomings and measured them against my goals and my future to take myself out of the running: Teachers are smart, I can't be a teacher because I'm not that smart.

Since I was at a loss for my future direction, I was in search of mentors and people who I could look up to. Masculinity and manhood was what I wanted. I desired a family, marriage, and the white picket fence. Yet, in the projects, I had no idea what that looked like. I admired my cousin Sean, the barber, since he made a lot of money. I wanted to be a married man like the men at church.

I gleaned what I could about manhood from my cousin Sean, men at church, and my friend, Alfonso a graduate from Seton Hall. I read any book Alfonso recommended. Alfonso and Mr. Howard recommended books like Malcolm X, Kirk Franklin, Langston Hughes, Alice Walker and a bunch of other authors. They were adamant about teaching me my history and showing me the way.

The more I was exposed to other environments, thought processes, and learned about the greatness of our people, I found myself standing out more from those closest to me. I was always different from my siblings and cousins. My brother Kayvon was always mischievous but good with his hands. When he was young, he was the only one who could fix the remote control. Kameisha has a kind heart. She loves to make sure people are taken care of. She will give you her last and borrow from someone to make sure you are good. Most of my cousins are cool. Many of my friends who connect with my family love my cousins because they are welcoming, with nice smiles and have inclusive personalities. I took on the role as a problem-solver early on. I wanted to solve whatever issues I saw in the family. Why are we always borrowing ketchup? What could we do better to stop this common occurrence?

When I was in college, Kayvon was in high school and he wanted to drop out with only one semester to go. I called an adult school and pretended to be him and set up a test so that he could go there and finish the year out. He never finished and was adamant about not finishing school. He is currently locked up. I had a cousin who failed the drivers test six or seven times. I got up one morning and I went to her house and we studied and my cousin passed that same day. I used to perm my aunts and cousins hair. I remember not using gloves and having pink and brittle nails for a few days. I could also fix a door that came off the hinges. Whatever was needed, I made sure it happened. It clearly translated into my adult life.

The X Factor

The Number System: Rationality

You + Belief in Yourself= The Answer

The majority of my childhood experiences growing up in the hood were irrational. Nothing really made sense to better yourself as a human being. It was more of, "this is what we do." People actually looked down on you if you went to school or worked a respectable job. Most people proudly said, "I'm just keepin' it real!" I never really understood that. To me, it appeared that dudes were literally copying other dudes and saying that *he* was "keepin' it real." The peer pressure of being down, cool, a thug, hustler, and a byproduct of your environment was so strong, that no one seemed to give a thought to "Who am I really?" "What do I want to do with my life?" Even though I was critical of my shortcomings, no pun intended, I was actually content being me.

The more knowledge I received, the stronger the desire I had to educate students and not indoctrinate them. In other words, I never wanted to tell kids what to do. Instead, I wanted to put them in situations to use their decision-making skills and thought process to determine the best outcome. I have spoken about ways to improve education with Core Group in South Africa and other forums in the community. I have worked with Hip Hop Education and had discussions with like-minded individuals. I strongly believe that the world would be better off if Black men are counted in the number if you will.

We need to exercise our brains more. We should be asking young people what problems they want to solve. Not what they want to be when they grow up. It restricts them as millennials are not wired that way. Solving problems outside of my home environment would have been beneficial to me in my upbringing. I am passionate about education and how it is done. I traveled as an Educational Socialist and went around the world and provided suggestions on how to improve education for Black and Latino young men who are at the bottom of the totem pole statistically speaking.

I desire to be a world changer. True world changers or true people are those who impact generations like Dr. Martin Luther King Jr. and Mahatma Gandhi. Both of these men sought to solve issues that were complex world problems. Dr. King was an orator making $200 year, but when he looked at the social work of injustice it was a huge task that needed to be addressed. He could have gone down as one of the greatest preachers, but his calling and ability to impact a generation, required his skills to solve the problems that affected generations.

I am also an advocate for Jaime Casap, Google's Global Educational Evangelist who is spearheading change in the culture of innovation and learning. He is convinced that education needs to reflect what is going on in the economy and the world. It must involve more critical thinking problem solving. Casap himself was born to a single mother in Hell's Kitchen, New York and he used education as his way out. Change can happen if we shift our views of learning in the classroom versus learning from the world around us.

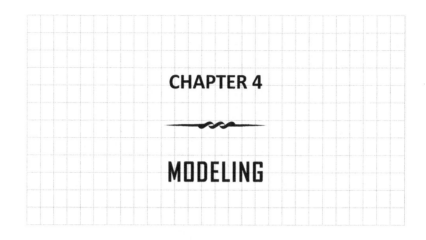

CHAPTER 4

MODELING

Choices, Assumptions & Approximations

Rumor had it that we made it. Just like *The Jeffersons*! I wish. The first time we moved was because Mommy was trying to do better and get us out of the PJ's. It was such a big deal in our family and friend circles. She was the first of her friends to escape. I was around seven years old when we moved uptown to Grant Avenue. The positive consensus concerning my mother was "She had two kids by this guy, he got her out of the projects *and* she's driving!" Everyone talked about us making it out or living the high life if you will.

If truth be told, we lived in a railroad shotgun apartment, which meant that you could see the entire apartment when you stood in one area of the living room. It was so tiny. The bathroom was literally in the kitchen. My mom was always yelling at one of us, "Close the got-damn door!"

We now lived uptown and the reputation was that it was bad. Downtown was more family oriented. My mom told us, "If you mind your business, you will be fine." It was not as dangerous as I thought, but I never found the camaraderie like I did in the projects. One of the uptown hangouts was Jimmy "The Cat" Dupree's boxing gym on MLK Drive.

Within the year we had a devastating fire. The next door neighbor's relative was playing with matches and the carpet caught on fire and spread to our apartment. We lived on the third floor. Cousin Allen, my mom's godfather came to visit that day and he told me to run downstairs. I remember all I had on was beige long johns and a white T-shirt. It was winter and it had just snowed. I stood outside looking up at the window yelling for my mother. Kayvon and Kamiesha were also still inside. Residents were outside looking on or trying to help.

One of the neighbors climbed onto the ledge of the building, near a second-floor window. He could see Mommy standing in front of her bedroom window, where the smoke was escaping. "Throw the kids!" he yelled frantically. Mommy threw Kayvon out first. The man caught him and threw him to another neighbor who was on the ground. Mommy threw Kameisha out next and the neighbor also tossed her to the man on the ground. I immediately grabbed my brother and sister's hands as I was hopping back and forth, barefoot in the three inches of snow.

The fire was very dramatic as we lost everything. The Red Cross came in and helped us. During that time my mom was talking to people on the phone all day. Every time I inquired she said it was the Red Cross. When Kenny got home, he went back into the apartment to look for the money he had stashed. Surprisingly, it was still there. He hadn't even checked to see if Mommy was alright. After the fire, he started keeping his money in a safe. Most of my family felt like my mother should have divorced him a while back. I believe she stayed with him because she wanted to make it work since no one believed they should be together. It was as if she was always trying to prove she was worthy to be with *him*, even though she called him a piece of sh__ to his face.

There is no greater loss than having a fire. We had absolutely nothing but the clothes on our backs. It was difficult having to ask others for common things that we had days before. Our housing, morning routines like brushing our teeth and eating breakfast were all compromised because of the fire.

After the fire, we went back to Booker T. for a few months because everything was destroyed. I periodically met up with Lewis at A&S store since he still lived in Lafayette. I got to stay with him only when Aunt Dolores was home, whom my mother loved. Lewis' place was filthy and roach-infested. It had a strong stench of old cigarettes and was unkempt.

Later, the Red Cross helped us relocate to a basement apartment on Bostwick Avenue, which was uptown. I lived there from second to fifth grade. When I think of my childhood, I think of Bostwick. It was the first place where my neighbor had me climb a gate to grab a switch off the tree so she could beat me, at the tender age of eight. Mommy gave permission to the neighbor, family, and my teachers to discipline me. She was serious about that "Mama Bear" thing.

Uptown was definitely more hood. Safety was a huge concern. Mommy dropped us off at Booker T. to visit Aunt Lorraine's every weekend so we could go outside and play with our cousins. Aunt Diane lived in Montgomery projects, which weren't too far, so her kids came over to Booker T. and played with us also. The Montgomery projects were the ones where people regularly got robbed and the elevator smelled like piss. Booker T. and Lafayette weren't as bad. If we were at home, we usually stayed in the house, unless it was summer time.

When the rest of the Spears family came out to Bostwick, the parents sat outside drinking and the kids played in the street. I got my street-sense and street-cred from living on Bostwick. In the late 80's/early 90's the area was called "The Hill." There was a lot of violence and murders occurring at the time. Being able to navigate through it all meant life or death. I was constantly thinking to myself, *I'm not gonna go down this block today because that happened last week. I'm not gonna walk on this street because this family is known to fight that family. I might not hanging with them because I know what they're into after school.* Being able to play in the projects during this time meant protection, familiarity, people, and community, so there was a safety net.

During the summer before fourth grade, there was an "Apollo" type talent show between Bostwick and Myrtle Ave. We used an abandoned building as the recreational area. Mommy stayed at home while I went to participate in the dance contest. All of the kids were separated by grade. As my group (third graders) were dancing, the emcee started pushing kids out of the way like he was the "Sandman." I was dancing so hard I was sweating. I saw the emcee headed towards my direction but I was still standing, going off. The emcee announced the runner-up and I won first place! We both received trophies but the mother of the runner-up came over and switched our trophies. I felt robbed. I went home and told Mommy, "I really won first place but I got *this* trophy." "Why?" she asked. "Cuz this lady took it from me," I responded half-jokingly. I didn't want to make a big deal because my mother would've fought that lady and got the trophy back. The whole event would've been ruined. There were a lot of things I downplayed because my mother would've Blacked out.

Young, Gifted and Black

Summertime jump-started my entrepreneurial spirit. I bought Kool-Aid and sugar to sell as "Frozen Icees" for a quarter a piece. I created signs and kids came through on the regular. Uncle Speed, Kenny's brother, asked me how much I made daily. "Did you subtract the money you spent on the product?" "What chu mean?" I asked confused. He taught me about business and even how to dress. Despite his lack, he was able to help me grow and optimize my abilities. I don't remember buying anything significant with the money I made, but I felt like a man. These were cornerstones in my life which showed me that I had something to offer. They confirmed in my spirit that I was going somewhere and that I couldn't just settle for whatever everyone else was doing.

I loved learning across the board, but especially math. I became a people person and enjoyed the extra-curricular activities I was exposed to at school such as acting, and the poetry and social studies clubs. I attended math and science academies on Saturdays. I kept myself preoccupied because I was running from Mommy's crazy antics. I met one of my early mentors, Mr. Donald Howard, my sixth grade English teacher. He took my fellow students and myself to his home and treated us like family. He saw our potential, but I knew I was his "golden child."

Sixth grade also introduced me to Shakespearean plays. I acted in "Romeo and Juliet" that year. Since I was a high achiever and had excellent grades, my teachers really embraced me. Mommy encouraged me to "work with computers" or to become a Certified Public Accountant since that's what my cousin did for a living. I remember studying very hard for an African-American Bee. It was like a spelling bee, but for African-American history. I knocked my opponents out the box! I was great at competing and dealing with pressure. Knowing Black people and their contributions to the world was something that came natural to me. It's the type of knowledge and information that still ignites me.

I performed my last Shakespearean play, *A Midsummer Night's Dream*, in middle school during my eighth grade year. I received a scholarship to attend Drew University for Shakespearean plays but didn't accept it. Church was a part of my everyday life since I was in the choir and was always at rehearsal or singing at different services. There was an older man, Alfonso Williams III, who attended my church and became another mentor in my life. He was interested in one of the Sunday school teachers, so that's how I actually picked up cues on how to treat a woman.

Things started to get better at home with Kenny. I didn't realize it at the time, but he had added value to our family dynamic. We always had cars and he tried to teach us about how they worked. The first time I legally drove was with him. Kenny invited us into his room when he was watching sports. He validated my actions and made things a big deal around his family and friends. With his fast southern drawl, he'd say, "Lewis got a lot of gotdamn girlfriends!"

When I was only 14, I danced really well, so he had me perform in front of the family. He recognized me in a lot of ways that my mother couldn't. She was familiar with my accomplishments so she'd say, "Yeah, OK. You always do that." Mommy rewarded me with things. On the other hand, Kenny rewarded me with affirmation. When it came to fighting, he encouraged me, "Boy, you better go fight!" He gave me the willpower that I needed.

Growing in Stature

Every time I felt settled and navigated my way through the neighborhood we'd move again. I didn't know what to feel. I moved from Grant, Bostwick, and then Harmon. I felt like, *whatever, I'm just not going to make any new friends. For what?* I was around 11 when we moved downtown to Harmon Street. We went from living in a basement apartment to living in a house. Although we were renting, it *felt* like ours. We could walk to Booker T Projects on the weekends and have good times with our friends. My cousins and I were in walking distance of each other's houses. I started sixth grade at a new school, PS 14, and was doing well academically and socially.

It was definitely an upgrade. We lived in a row of houses that were connected, so it was a true neighborhood. Although Bostwick *looked* like a neighborhood, it was far from it. On Bostwick, we heard about people getting stabbed or jumped around the Hill. Once we moved to Harmon, our family seemed more solidified.

I was always in charge of Kayvon and Kamiesha. We were latchkey kids, so I was really the authoritarian in their lives. Middle school helped me to gain an even greater sense of independence since I started going to people's houses who were outside of my family, which was a big deal since my mother trusted no one. Prior to this, I had only spent the night at my cousin's house.

Church attendance became a regular part of my life. Granddaddy picked me up for church but he was inconsistent. My cousin Tiffany and I were really close growing up. I remember looking up her skirt one time when I was real young. She ran and told Grandma, who smacked the mess out of me. Thankfully, our relationship recovered. She lived with her paternal grandmother, and was about two years older than me, so I hung onto every word she spoke. She was very pretty, with long hair and a small frame. All the guys liked her. Tiffany was smart too, a real go-getter, but spoiled.

She came to visit one Thanksgiving and told me about the Baptist church she attended. "You should come to my church. We go on trips!" "For real?" I asked excitedly. "Yup, the van will come pick you up." I had not been to church in a while and was looking forward to a new church with new people. Tiffany's Uncle Eddie drove the van but he was an impatient dude. If I was running late, he was out! Mrs. Williams picked me up from time to time. One week, it was as if the church members had decided that Deacon Jones would be my new ride. Unlike Eddie, he was very patient. Deacon Jones picked me up every week and if I was just getting up when he arrived, he'd pick up everyone else on his route and then return for me. Deacon Jones drove with one hand in a stationary position on the wheel because he had a hand ailment and smoked a cigarette with the other. I guess the others got tired of coming to get me since I was always somewhere different, between Bostwick, Harmon, Booker T. and Montgomery projects. Kayvon and Kamiesha never came with me, except during Vacation Bible School in the Summer. Mommy's attitude was, "I'll let you try whatever you want until you don't want to do it anymore!"

One Summer evening in the seventh grade, Mommy and Kenny sat me down and calmly said, "We're getting a divorce. We can't do this anymore." I began questioning and counseling them through. I asked, "What makes it really bad? What are you missing out on? What is this going to do to the family? Ya'll been together this long- ya'll better figure it out." I don't know what hit home, but they stayed together for several more years.

This experience validated my ability to be a peacemaker and bring people together to help them gain a new perspective. It also scared me because I wondered what would happen if I wasn't present. I realized that I was a major contributor to our family dynamic and I was privy to a lot of adult business than I should have been. Mommy and Kenny shielded Kayvon and Kamiesha from plenty. I was very involved in the decision-making process with my mother when it came to my brother and sister. I'd tell her, "They're gonna go to this school; they should wear this; they should eat this; these are some of the things we should do together." I grew up quickly because I had no choice.

I was driving by the time I was 12 years old. Mommy was drinking more than usual and it became a a yo-yo habit. So

I'd have to take the wheel to get her home safely whenever she demanded. I recall driving her home while she was intoxicated, with Kayvon and Kamiesha in the back seat. It was late at night and less than a two mile drive, but I was driving, nonetheless. Mommy kept yelling at me, "Stay straight! Stay straight!"

Here I was being responsible, although I didn't really know what I was doing. Kenny had let me play around in the car with putting my foot on the brake and simple stuff like that back in the day, but now I was full-blown driving! I had to turn right onto Harmon where I could just pull into the parking spot. We walked up the block to get to the house. It was surreal. Anytime Mommy was drunk, her requests were ridiculous. She'd say things like, "Lewis, carry me on ya back so I can get to the car!" or if she was in the house, "Fix me some eggs. I need some eggs!" If I resisted or had an attitude, she'd go off, "Oh, what I do for you? Oh, I don't do nothing for you?" I always felt obligated to make sure that I took care of her. "Scrambled with no cheese, right Ma?"

The X Factor

You + Overcoming Obstacles = The Answer

Modeling Choices, Assumptions & Approximation
"No matter where you are from your dreams are valid."
Lupita Nyong'o

Often people try to write you off because you come from American urban communities. The reality is that surviving in your hood makes you more valuable in the world. Whatever you dream you can most assuredly do. Your work ethic is is the key to your success. You can navigate anything and any-place around the world.

I am reminded of one of the most memorable episodes of *A Different World*, when Dwayne and his best friend Ron were locked up with three white guys. They were arrested because they got into an altercation when they saw the guys spray painting Ron's car with the "N" word. During the jail scene, Dwayne and one guy are at each other's throat. The white guy goes on to brag about how his grandfather came to this country as an immigrant and could not speak English, yet worked hard to provide for his family.

Dwayne countered by saying that his grandfather was born here, fought for this country, and could not sit and have a cup of coffee in a diner. Dwayne continued to lament about the fact that no matter how many degrees he attains, white people will only see a Black face. This generation needs to talk about the propaganda and bureaucracy that revolves around the cultural insecurities and race. We need to bring an awareness of *A Different World* to this generation. That show tackled so many social issues, looked at nuances, and tried to find solutions to societal problems.

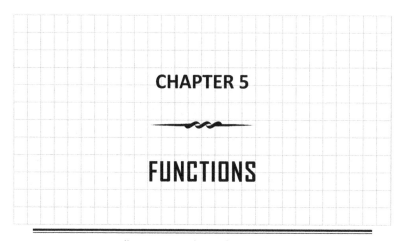

CHAPTER 5

FUNCTIONS

> " *Doing nothing for others*
> *is the undoing of ourselves."*
> **Horace Mann**

I was a classic teacher's pet. The kid who stayed after school to have discussions with the teacher and volunteer for any chores they needed. I had an inside track to what my teachers liked and disliked. I recall getting my first "C" for which Mommy had a stern talk with me even though she never helped me with my homework or any school project. Language Arts was very hard for me because words and literature were too confusing. There were always exceptions to weird rules and nothing made sense. I had a difficult time pronouncing words so I began studying people by watching their demeanor and listening to every word they uttered. Math was second nature to me and I loved numbers because they made sense. Math was one of the very few things in life that was always true.

People usually favored me and God always placed people in my life who took care of me. Whether they were from school, church, or the community, I usually had someone looking out. Kabili Tayari was a huge influence on me as a young boy. He was president of the youth task force of the NAACP. He was adamant about showing up and doing his part by being a positive force in the lives of young people in the inner city. He took several of us to empowerment conferences as well as overnight retreats. I became involved in the Boys and Girls Club and attended events at the New Jersey Black Issues Committee, that included influential members such as Queen Latifah.

Clownin' Around

I spent a lot of time with my homegirl, Shelly. Her father was a crackhead and was in and out of jail for stealing. My best friend was a Puerto-Rican named Elliot. He was a year older than me and had been left back. He was my dude because we were always on the same wavelength. We were both Christians and his mother actually drove the church van. Elliot was pudgy because his mom cooked all the time. His father was a handyman and had a shop in his house where he taught us how to build and fix things. Elliot and I worked on school projects together. His two sisters were in the same grades as Kayvon and Kamiesha, so the younger kids were always around too. Elliot's family taught us Spanish and I loved eating their food.

When Elliot's mom picked me up for church, she spoke English on the bus so I wouldn't feel as if they were talking about me. I wasn't thinking about that - I loved going to Elliot's to eat and do my homework. Mommy loved their family too. Elliot's parents had been together forever. The picture of their family was projected onto mine. Elliot's family assumed that my family was just like theirs; they didn't know that Kenny wasn't my biological father. Elliot knew, but he was big on protecting my image. He was intentional about presenting me in the best light to his parents instead of perpetuating the negative stereotype that Blacks were dysfunctional.

Our social studies teacher gave her phone number to students if they needed help. Elliot and I called her and asked a question. Before we hung up I said, "Elliot thinks you're crazy Miss Newsome!" Elliot was on the other line and yelled, "No I don't Miss Newsome!" The story was that she had lost her two children in a fire and went crazy after that. Miss Newsome hung up on us. She came to school the next day and made an announcement while she was eating her lunch during class. "There are two students in this class, I won't say their names, who won't *ever* get away with calling me and jerking around!" After that, she went back to eating her fried chicken. Elliot was sitting a few seats across from me but I wouldn't dare look at him, for fear of Miss Newsome breaking my neck! The fact that she was hurt over our actions made me feel so bad. She was my teacher through eighth grade, so she eventually got over it, thankfully.

Growing Pains

My mom was very passionate about her kids not embarrassing her in public. There was a time where mom had to pop my brother in Pathmark and someone called DYFS on her and once worker came she knew my mom and the worker closed the case and kept it moving. When they see how passionate she is about kids following rules and misbehaving, they know that her heart is in the right place. Yes, we were probably being mistreated at times, but mom was very nuturing, supportive, and loving. But don't be fooled, she would pop you in a minute!

We moved to Whiton Street when I was about 13. I was good in school but still a wreck at home. I'd yell at Mommy, "I don't know why you wit that man-he don't love you anyway!" She tore my behind up, but I didn't care. I just wanted to be heard. I remember Mommy hitting me with the phone while she was on it. I said something smart so she back-handed me with the phone and then brought it back up to her face and said, "Hello?" Heck no, you done broke my phone!" I let loose because I couldn't stand Kenny. Some days I just yelled to the top of my lungs, "I don't have to listen to him. He ain't my father!"

My first house parties were at Darnell's in Booker T. We had to pay a dollar to get in. To my dismay, none of the girls were giving me play! They all said the worst thing a girl can say to a teenage boy, "Yo, Lewis you're like our little brother. What are you doing here?" What they were really saying was, "You're a goody two-shoes. You're a kid who gets good grades." They were drinking, smoking weed, and more. This was also the beginning of my "short" complex. I went to a total of three parties from ages 13-15. Each time I went I felt ostracized, like I didn't belong there. Thankfully, my lack of partying didn't ruin my social life. I frequented Jackson Ave. a.k.a. MLK Avenue (every urban community has an avenue they renamed "MLK"). It was the avenue that you took to get to anywhere in the city. You knew people were going to be there, so you'd rock your best gear since they'd be watching.

I continued acting when I went to James J. Ferris High School. By sophomore year, I was third lead and was confident that I'd be first the following year, but when junior year rolled around, the program was dismantled due to a lack of funding. After that, I lost interest in acting.

On the marriage front, Mommy and Kenny weren't doing well at all. They were at a card game and she told Kenny (in front of other people) that there was a guy at her job who she liked and planned on sleeping with. Mommy didn't back down. "You're weak! I stayed with you when you cheated on me." I read her journals when I was 15. They expressed how insignificant she felt. I held a lot of resentment towards my mother. I finally mustered the courage to ask her, "Were you not thinking? Did you not know who you were going to have me with?" She just looked at me, so I left the room. I didn't know if I was going to get hit or if she was going to scream or cry. I didn't know what her reaction would be but for some reason, I had to ask. Mommy was really down after that. I think she sensed I was raising a genuine question and not coming from a disrespectful or spiteful place.

You + Using Resources = The Answer

What's that in your hand?[2] I don't think we realize the wealth of assets available to us right within our reach. Oftentimes, what we need to get ahead or to provide us with a new perspective of our situation is nearby. In my youth, I did not realize the value of a recommendation from a teacher, community leader, pastor, or even grocery store owner. There is always someone who either has what you need or is connected to someone who can provide it to you. People are resources, so use them wisely.

I encourage you to take advantage of an opportunity to immerse yourself into a new environment. Even if it is just for a day. Take a trip to the zoo, a museum, a local theater, a college campus or an extended trip to visit a family member. I recall the summer before seventh grade when I went to visit my great Uncle Robert (Grandma Grum's brother) in Texas. I was supposed stay for two months, but I ended up coming back after about two weeks because I was a punk. I had my own room (which I didn't even have at home), but I couldn't take it. In my mind, Texas was too slow. I later realized that I was immature and naive. I never gave my new

---

2 Exodus 4:2

environment a chance. I was so comfortable in my dysfunctional home and hood surroundings, that I was like a fish out of water in the beauty, quiet, and open space that Texas had to offer. All those years I stressed about not getting a good night's sleep because of the constant visitors in my home or the loud outside activities. Imagine the new friends I could have made in two months? Imagine what I could have learned from my elder Uncle? Instead of convincing myself that I missed home, I actually missed out on connections and growth. Don't shy away from exposure to new opportunities because they could be the missing link to help you solve a problem, discover an innate gift, or steer you in the direction for your purpose. Whatever you need to move forward in life is within your reach, go out and grab it!

2nd Marking Period

THE AWAKENING:
Rutgers University

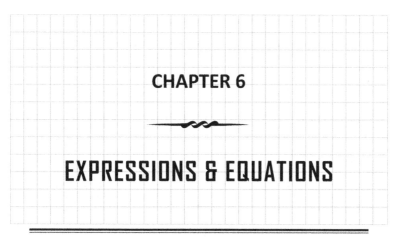

CHAPTER 6

EXPRESSIONS & EQUATIONS

*"None of us is as
smart as all of us."*
Ken Blanchard

When I arrived at Rutgers University in 2001, I chose to major in math. Unfortunately, I was struggling in *all* of my math courses but hesitated to ask for help because I didn't want to be exposed. *I was supposed to know this stuff.* I participated in the Educational Opportunity Fund Program (EOF), which was a scholarship to improve access to higher education for low-income and first generation college students. The great thing was that the EOF provided counseling and tutoring. I finally got up the nerve to go. It was cool being with Black people who looked like me. The counselors understood our struggles and helped us connect with tutors. They also connected us to one another so we could learn from each other's strengths. We had to meet the grade criteria and partake in certain extra-curricular activities. The goal was to close the achievement gap. Initially, we took summer courses to catch up.

I started off low in the math and english courses. I was grateful to have plenty of support from the counselors, tutors and my classmates. I also participated in the Rutgers Liberated University Choir as well as serving as a peer-mediator group, where we came up with ideas for different events. I created a world that made sense to me so I could thrive in it and not feel worthless. It was a common thing for me to do. Whenever I felt disenfranchised or less-than, I created a new world that made me feel alive. It was a defense mechanism I developed as a result of growing up in the projects.

There was always an air of "You have to do better," at Rutgers. I had never interacted with white people on a regular basis. I went to an all-Black elementary school and a Black and Latino high school. I started taking classes with friends or "Black courses" because I knew other Blacks would be present. It was a culture shock to go to college and be thrown into classrooms with nothing but white students. I had never heard of bayous and cul-de-sacs. I was used to community pools and dead ends. It seemed like the knowledge of bayous and cul-de-sacs was more relevant than what I was used to. If whites were speaking my language, it would have been the norm.

Three of my friends and I had all attended Ferris High School and were in Magnet programs, which meant that we were selected because we were the top students in Jersey City. At Rutgers freshman orientation, the Dean uttered those famous words spoken by most deans at the beginning of the school year, "Look to your left, look to your right. Some of these people may not be here for graduation." When I graduated in 2006, LaShell and Martin weren't present. I went on to graduate from New Jersey City University with my Masters in Urban Education in 2009. All I got from my family was a "Congratulations!" I had to throw my own party! My cousin Jalil was released from jail around the same time and he received a homecoming fit for a king. My family bought him Tims and made sure he was G'd up after stepping out of the joint.

The more I was exposed to in college, I drew a wedge between my family and myself. I began to look at them with a judgmental eye. I asked "What's *wrong* with you?" I asked my mother again, "You didn't think about having me with another man? You didn't think about him being a loser?" I had grown to believe that when I decided to have kids I was going to put them in the best position possible. I began questioning everything about my upbringing. *Why were our lights off if you were working two jobs? Why did I have to be embarrassed going to the store with food stamps? Why did we have to be on government assistance?* I was about 19 years old when I asked my mother these questions. She had a hard time pronouncing words but still cursed me out. "Oh, so I'm not good enough to be on your quote- leveral [level]-end quote?" My mother was unfiltered.

I used school as a scapegoat to deal with all of the chaos and family problems in my life. I began harvesting a skillset of problem-solving and developed a sense of self and individuality. My stress and anxieties about not being good enough appeared every now and then, but I was beginning to understand that it was OK.

Letting Go to Grow

Pressure at school to perform at a high level and dysfunction at home began to mount. I started feeling like something was wrong with me. It was overwhelming living two lifestyles; being one way at school and another way around my family. A pastor at church recommended I see a therapist. I was apprehensive at first. I started going and then I was uncomfortable. I'd stop and start several times, switching therapists along the way. I am now with my guy Armando, and life is good.

Therapy has been the most important step in my healing process. I knew that I had a lot of hatred in my heart towards my father. I hadn't seen him in a long time and one day I ended up driving behind him as he was driving the school bus. I didn't realize it was him at first. I was frustrated with sitting in traffic and started spewing out commands of where I wanted him to turn the bus. As I was navigating the route in my head, my father started moving according to what I was saying. It was surreal. I understood where my reasoning came from.

When I finally decided to reconnect with my father, I struggled in the beginning. I felt like I was doing something against my mother since she was the one who devoted her entire life to me and contributed to my success. I had just began my teaching career in math and my mother was furious. "Nah, forget him! Where was he when our lights was off?" I was conflicted. A part of me was like, "For real son!" But I had to do what was right for *me*. Sometimes we adopt the attitude of our parents which can be either good or bad. They don't even have to say anything, but because we *know* them, we can read their emotions.

When I went to see Lewis, I told him that he abandoned me. He rebuked me with, "No, I bought you that Nintendo when you was nine!" I couldn't believe he was serious. "Yo, you gon' bring that up?" I was expecting to hear something along the lines of "I'm sorry. I was the worst parent in the world. I'll never do it again." I had to face reality. He wasn't going to say, "I love you," so I studied his love language. My father loved me the way he knew to love me. Although it seemed to be missing at first, I came to understand how he loved. He called me one day to tell me to bring my clothes to his house so he could wash them. He didn't have a dryer. He hung my clothes around his house, so they smelled like cigarettes. The fact that he did it for me was enough.

He began calling me on Sundays to talk about football and I'm not a football guy. He taught me about the game over the phone. In the beginning, if I would've waited for him to say he loved me, I wasn't going to get it. Saying I love you is so natural for me because it is how my mom raised us. Lewis was a loving and accommodating guy, yet we had not built up our adult relationship for him to feel comfortable saying those impactful three words. I sought him out to get something from him. I wanted to show him who I was. I just felt like to know me was a gift, even as narcissistic as it may sound. If I didn't humble myself to form a relationship with my father, I would've missed out on a whole side of myself. Getting to know him made me feel like a whole person. I felt authentic. It was a revelation like, *that's where I get this from. Now I can go forth*!

Failing to reconcile with an absentee parent is a process we can't take for granted. *What if your father's objective was only to bring you into the world? He did his part. Are you going to punish him for not being in your life? And how are you punishing him (if you're hating him from a distance and he doesn't know it)? You're drinking poison and expecting him to die?* You need to liberate yourself. It's not easy, but you're going to have to denounce the ideas you have in your head concerning father-son and mother-daughter relationships. You'll have to build a relationship with "this person." The ultimate goal is to understand who you are because of them.

Scarlet Doubts

I harbored negative thoughts and feelings of not cutting the mustard throughout college. During one session, my therapist asked me to write myself a letter. It felt strange at first, but once I got through the first paragraph, the words just flowed.

A letter to my young self,

Listen man, you hang tough because I got you. I won't let nothing happened to you. Just because your experiences were limited and very challenging, it doesn't mean that you were devalued in anyway. It actually means all of your experiences and your hard work is going to allow you to move forward and be more equipped for life.

God is not going to leave you. The Bible says he would never leave you nor forsake you, and I want you to hold on to that. You don't have to be insecure about anything. Your personality, your charisma, your wit, and your ability to develop people and yourself is an amazing feat. Don't think that you are short-changing yourself. I know that you cry and feel depressed when you aren't able to live out your life wholly. Just relax you got this.

I know the environment you're in makes you feel really uncomfortable and really unsafe, but if you continue to work hard you will be able to live anywhere you want to live. You don't have to be like all of the boys in the community because you aren't like them. That's what sets you apart. I know it'll be nice if all the girls liked you and you were popular, but it's OK. You have plenty of time for girls.

I know you're wondering why your life has to be this hard, but it is definitely going to teach you a lot about life's requirements. Take your time, you got this. Don't underestimate your journey. Believe me you're gonna be fine. You have family and friends who are committed to your growth. Read more and study harder. Lean on God more, since you can't do this alone. Focus on those things that are going to develop you into a purposeful, well intentioned individual.

There's a world of opportunities waiting to be explored. Continue to look for moments to cherish life. You are not missing anything by focusing on the intangibles. In fact, you're increasing your value because you are focusing on the things that man cannot see. There are richer, more meaningful things on the inside. Remember to hang in there, because I love you.

The One

During my freshman year I spotted my future wife, Myriam. I tried to date her but she dissed me! She felt I wasn't mature enough and that I wasn't a man of God. I never really thought I deserved her. She was definitely my "reach girl," but she finally obliged to dating me during my senior year. We did a lot of fun stuff like bowling and roller skating. Myriam graduated in May 2005 and moved back home in June. We hung out after we both finished school. I stayed an extra semester to get more credits in math. Myriam worked for one year and then she began medical school. I thought her parents, Joseph and Jacqueline, hated me when we first got together. You see, Myriam is Haitian-American. I'm JB-Just Black. Myriam had her own car and was driving us all over the place when we started dating. I didn't have a car. I also had locks in my hair at the time, which represented the antithesis of what her parents raised their kids to think was respectable. I represented the "Black boy" or "vaga-bone" (vagabond) as they would say.

Growing up, Myriam was instructed, "You need to separate yourself from them. You look alike, but you're not the same." Myriam didn't care about how her parents felt about me. She stood by me and defended me. While our love was blooming, Mommy and Kenny's had finally come to a head. They separated, which was a big move for my mother. After Kenny left, she was evidently happier. She came alive.

When I took Myriam to meet my mother, we walked into her apartment and the door was open. Anyone who lives in the house knows that if the door is open, someone's home; if it's closed, then no one's home. *I* knew my mother was in there, but Myriam didn't. She didn't see her, so my mom yelled, "Who dat? Why didn't she speak? Oh, she's rude!" I'm like, "Wait Ma-she didn't see you!" I diffused the situation and told Myriam, "That's not what she meant." When we got in the car to go home I reassured her. "My mom's really a nice person. I'm sorry." I didn't know what to tell her. It was Myriam's introduction to what my whole life had been.

There was a lot of me bridging the gap between my two worlds in the beginning of our relationship because my mother usually went too far. Myriam was always reserved but willing to fight for what she believed in. I guess she didn't think that was a battle worth fighting since it was her first time meeting my mother. There were some crazy things my mom hated and not speaking was one of them. If she said, "Hi, how you doin?" to someone and they waved at her, she'd boldly ask, "Did I wave at you?" Growing up, my friends greeted her with a, "Hi, Mrs. White," and she got upset. "*Mrs. White?* Do I look like my mother-in-law? Do I look old to you? I ain't old, call me Regina." Now everyone else's mom wanted to be called "Mrs. So-and-so," but *my* mother had a problem with that.

So when I knew I was ready to get married, I asked Myriam's father Joseph for her hand in marriage. Once we were engaged, Jacqueline continued to ask Myriam, "Why are you connected to that man?" However, she was always cordial face-to-face. I would tell Myriam, "I don't care, I have a lot of people who love me." Asking for a girls hand in marriage was something that I saw on TV and I did not know what I was doing. I called Myriam's sister Ginnie, so she could buffer this awkward conversation. She did a good job of being the liaison between me and her parents. I remember sitting there and her uncle from Haiti was there and he made it worse and he said well how come your family is not here? I made some excuse and tried to change the subject.

Myriam's father Joseph was a bit more laid back, but appeared ambivalent. One of the stipulations for me to obtain his blessing to marry Myriam was for him to meet my parents. I asked my mom, "Who you want me to bring to dinner, my Dad or your husband?" "I really don't want you to bring either one cuz they're both annoying," she said seriously. She settled for Kenny. "I can stomach him." According to my mother and the family, Myriam was high-sadiddy, with her pinky in the air. When my mother walked into Myriam's parents' house she mumbled, "She talkin 'bout me and they livin like *this*?" Myriam's parents were very simple people. They didn't really buy themselves clothes. They didn't even have cable. My mom was cracking on their shoes and everything, but she liked their food.

For as long as I could remember, Mommy loved to have a cigarette after eating, which was a piece of information she chose to volunteer. It was a point of judgment. "Yeah, I smoke but I asked God to take the taste out of my mouth." Jacqueline and her sister told my mother they would pray for her. Ginnie was laughing the whole time. Mommy continued, "I ask God to take the taste out my mouth. My God is good." I'm thinking, "Mom, you go to church like once every three months." Overall, I think they sensed the closeness of our relationship. We were buggin' out throughout dinner. During this time, Mommy was cheating on Kenny. She blurted out, "Lewis' dad look like..." I had to interrupt with a quick, "Ma, stop!"

As Myriam and I got closer to marriage, I wasn't sure what to expect. She had grown up in a two-parent household. I didn't know what it was like for the man to be the head. Kenny usually worked nights. He and Mommy did everything differently. I asked Myriam how we would move forward. I knew she wanted to become a doctor. She confidently said "I'll give you my paycheck, as long as I have what I need. I'll take care of the family." I assumed that whoever made the most money wore the pants. I didn't realize I felt that way until right before we got married.

I was insecure about the fact that she would eventually make more money than me. Mommy and Kenny's money was separate and they always fought. I wanted something different. I decided to set myself up for a functional relationship by agreeing to participate in pre-marital classes at our home church, Abundant Life Family Worship Church, in New Brunswick, New Jersey. We also made it a point to seek out people who were in whole marital relationships. I reached out to Alfonso from my former church and his wife. In addition, we joined the marriage ministry at our church and connected with seasoned couples who mentored us along our journey.

Myriam and I got married May 7, 2010. When we first got together we agreed that the hierarchy of our relationship would be, God first, career second and relationship third. We were both at a point in our lives where our career aspirations required a great deal of focus, and we pushed and supported each other to be the best that we could be. We prayed each night on the phone before we got married. We are both busy, especially as new parents, and we are still finding how to balance it all.

Early in the marriage, there were times I would wild out, which gave Ginnie and her husband reason to believe I was a "wild boy," but Ginnie's husband was the same way. However, he didn't get the same flack that I did because he's Haitian. In the beginning of our marriage, I told my mother that Myriam's fear was that she would overstep her boundaries. I was direct by encouraging them to get together, "You're my wife-you're my mom, ya'll need to figure this out." They discussed it over lunch and gained clarity. My mother gave us the freedom to be us. My family is so close-knit, that we had family meetings, once a week on Sundays. We focused on whatever the family needed first and if our spouses didn't like it, it was too bad. My family always had a great need. Myriam is very low-maintenance. All she needs is a couch and a magazine, so I had a habit of dropping everything to make sure my family was OK. My family trusted me to take care of them, yet I had to recognize the necessity of putting my wife first.

Although my cousin Tiffany and I grew apart, I became close to her sister, Tamika. Everyone in my family envies our relationship. She gets stuff my own sister doesn't. Kamiesha and I have always had a father-daughter relationship since I was always watching over her and Kayvon. I took her out when she was younger and spent time with her. I let her know what I thought of her. I often said, "You're beautiful. You have what it takes to succeed." This is how my relationship with Kamiesha differed from her relationship with her father. However, we're starting to develop a real brother-sister relationship.

It's great that my sister and I talk a lot more and talk about relationship things and we talk every day because of our kids.

My son AJ asks to speak to my nephew often. We also talk about things that are hurting us or things that we are excited about. Her son stayed with me for a couple of days and he cried because he missed his mom. I told him one evening, "shut your mouth!" Now it is a running joke between us. She asks him. "what does uncle Lewis say to you?" He responds, "uncle Lewis says, shut your mouth!"

You + Asking for Help = The Answer

I've found that it takes courage and strength to ask for help. It is not a sign of weakness or incompetency. Most of the time our pride gets in the way and we end up stressed out trying to be superman or superwoman to cover up our insecurities. You cannot do everything, be everything, and know everything. For those of you who think you have the secret to being the end-all, you are headed for an eventual crash and burn.

When I first got to Rutgers, my grades suffered because I was too embarrassed to get help from the counselors and tutors whose sole purpose was to help me. Once I realized that there were others who needed help, then I was able to be fully honest with my needs, and fill any inadequacies. The knowledge-sharing and working with others took my math aptitude to a new level. I've always loved math and gravitated toward numbers, but now I saw numbers in an entirely new light. That's when I knew I would eventually pursue math and education as a career.

In addition, recognizing and accepting the fact that I needed therapy to help me cope with my past, present, and future was life-changing. Mental illness is an unchecked disease in Black communities. The stigma of therapy and acknowledging that you are struggling in certain areas in your mind must be reversed. So many people could be helped if they changed their perspective on seeking help to handle everyday life challenges.

Another aspect in asking for help that I failed to recognize until recently is that people genuinely want to help you if they have what you need. Therefore, when someone is providing knowledge or impacting your day, that person is being fulfilled. It's like you are building them up as they are building you up. Also, when you ask others for help you are demonstrating that you value their abilities, you trust them, and you are willing to be vulnerable. Too many times we have our guard up because we fear rejection or fear that we are much better on paper than in person. No matter what the circumstances, always know that you have something to offer to the situation.

I strongly believe that we are our brothers and sisters' keeper's. We should have honest evaluations of ourselves and seek to do better to help bring others up. Whether it's our family, friends, or anyone connected to us, we all have a part to play in each other's growth. My wife and I have made it our job to create a safe non-judgemental zone in our family meetings. We ensure that everyone knows we support them no matter what. I am intentional and carve out time to express love. I love it when Mom just calls and shares stories. These are the types of interactions that I hold near and dear to my heart. Love is what love does. Call your family or friend to tell them that you love them. Pick up their favorite snack when you are out shopping for yourself. Text them to remind them that a show is coming on soon, or a new book just dropped, or about an upcoming event that interests them. All of these things will show you care. And while you are helping others, you will see how much more confident you are when you ask others for help. Now that I have my own organization, there is no shame in my game in asking for help!

3rd Marking Period

THE BIG TEST: Harvard University

CHAPTER 7

———∿∿———

A Ram in the Bush

After graduating from Rutgers in 2006, I enrolled in New Jersey City University to begin the alternative program for teaching because I didn't have a teaching certification. At the time, Rutgers didn't offer a teaching program, but I knew that teaching was definitely my calling. I was a substitute teacher for a while and then got accepted into the Urban Education program. I ended up taking so many credits in the alternate program that I decided to get my master's degree which was only about 15 credits shy of obtaining my degree.

How on earth did I get to Harvard? Every time I think of this story, I realize that this experience is my reason for being and it was ignited by a desire to just love people and assume the best in everyone. My mantra has always been, "that's the best they can possibly do" and I assume the best of everyone in their situation for the most part.

One professor assigned groups for a project and in those groups we had to discuss ideas from the assignment. I cannot recall the actual topic, but I know that some people in the group were not actively engaged. I, on the other hand, took the assignment extremely serious because at least one part dealt with race. I really created something good and I provided my ideas on the topic to my group.

Looking back at that incident, the professor was basically scanning the room and walking around to hear different comments to see if there were any outliers that she needed to clarify or to validate any points or comments. I actually remember her walking near me and I was talking confidently about the topic. At the end of the class she suggested that we all write our *own* synopsis about it and send it to everybody else in the group. The paper was due a week later. I showed up to class and didn't complete my portion. I ended up looking at the assignment of my peer and because she said everything that I originally said in her paper. I erased her name, put my name at the top of her paper and hit send. I submitted this young lady's work as my own. I clearly PLAGIARIZED! What an embarrassment.

It became a huge issue because I felt that my peer stole my swag, my ideas, and my significance. I felt like she was Christopher Columbus and I was of Indian descent. But because she made a big deal about it, I felt horrible. I thought, "this behavior is punishable by expulsion, I can't be expelled." I had been an ideal student my entire career in terms of getting work done, making sure that I showed up not simply my presence, but intellectually, psychologically, and emotionally contributing. I took a great deal of pride in my work because that's all I had to prove who I was and what I could offer. You couldn't see my "greatness" by looking at my appearance because I didn't have much in terms of stature or material possessions.

All I had was my desire to do well and impress people with my intelligence and hard work. The young woman that I plagiarized sent me an email going off about what I had done. Rightfully so, and she sent an email to the teacher, threatening to go above her if necessary. I'm still uncertain of what she said in the email to me because we had spoken prior to me reading the email and she begged me to delete it without reading it. I remember feeling annoyed by her because she used all of my ideas. I should have drawn back a bit during the discussion in class. I said to myself, *I won't show up and allow these people to plagiarize my thoughts.*

I never communicated that I felt she took my thoughts, instead I was apologetic for what I had done because I just wanted it to be over. Here's where it gets interesting: The teacher requested a meeting with me and I went to her office prior to the incident and we had a great rapport. We talked privately about big ideas concerning education. I really thought I was summoned to her office to be kicked out of school. I knew that had to be one of the hardest conversations she had to have, considering I was the only Black male in the class. She informed me that she witnessed the entire interaction between me and the young lady on my team. She said to me, "I don't think that you are a cheater. I don't think that you're a liar. I've seen you over the past couple of months and I just think that you're overwhelmed with everything that you have to do."

It was as if a weight was lifted off my shoulders. I felt so light. I may have even seen the light, the sheer grace of God. No one had ever given me the benefit of the doubt like that especially at this level. My professor was a white woman. Not that race matters in this situation, because what I did was wrong. I was sure that she and the other lady who was also white would build an alliance and "gang" up on me to have me expelled. The professor, who is still one of my greatest influencers, heard the suggestions that I made in the group setting, and was very supportive of me and in the ideas that were innate in me.

As fate would have it, this is the same professor who referred me to Harvard. During one of our discussions months after the incident, she said, "Why don't you apply to the Harvard Doctoral program? You're about to graduate with your Masters. I think you should apply to the doctoral program." I'm thinking, *why is she presenting this idea in a such a jovial manner? I didn't think Harvard, with its reputation, would accept someone like me.* I replied, "Harvard! I would never get into Harvard!" "Well you won't know until you try," she added. "OK I'll apply, but you have to write me a recommendation letter." For a second, I felt a tingling inside, like I had a chance to get in because she had completed Harvard graduate school.

I went to the informational seminar and realized that I couldn't commit to the three-year Educational Doctorate Program (EDD) as my fiancé (at the time) and I were planning to get married in May of the following year. So instead of applying to the EDD program, I decided to commit to the one year School Leadership Master's Program. Myriam and I spoke about the possibilities of my acceptance and what it would do for our marriage. I suggested that we wait until after the Harvard graduation, whether it was one or three years, and she responded with a very strong "NO!" I knew I loved her and I didn't want to lose her, nor did I want to forgo this opportunity. I came up with a solution that allowed me to "have my cake and eat it too."

At that time, I had been working under a teaching contract since 2006 with the district teaching math for the first three years. The application process itself was challenging in that I wanted to put my best foot forward. While I felt encouraged to apply, I didn't think my credentials were good enough. The very thing that I led with in the past, my intelligence, is the same thing that would be crushed if I didn't get accepted.

I took the GRE which is like the SAT for graduate schools and I scored a little more than a thousand (on a 1600 scale). I had recommendation letters from my professor and also my principal, the essay I originally submitted was written back in undergrad while at Rutgers, which wasn't good enough.

I had a colleague who was a former journalist, and later became one of my dearest friends, look at the essay. She was extremely disappointed. She taught me skills and research techniques that I now use to apply to all of my jobs. She focused on the program expectations and used their words in my essay. We researched previous prolific attendees of Harvard, who beliefs mirrored mine. I was uncomfortable as she dissected the essay that I worked so hard to produce.

Here is an excerpt of my essay:

I've grown tired of being an anomaly. My hometown of Jersey City, NJ is a painful eyesore filled with stereotypical urban indiscretions. As a 6th grade teacher, I see children who lack the motivation to excel and are content with mediocrity. At the core of this problem are the parents who work for minimum wage depend on public assistance, have little or no education and can't fulfill their own aspirations. The problem is cyclic and parents and children alike are angry and disenchanted with the cycle, which leads them to fall victim to the drugs, crime, and gangs that plague our inner-city.

As an educator, I developed a keen awareness of the educational and emotional needs of urban youth, particularly Black males. I understand the harsh realities that they are faced with every day, because I faced those very same issues growing up.

Through Harvard University Graduate School of Education, I am eager to explore the advantages and disadvantages of a eurocentric frame of education for African American men. This is of particular interest to me because as a member of that demographic, I've often questioned the effectiveness of the type of education and if an afrocentric education would encourage African American males to pursue and attain higher education.

In, **The Souls of Black Folk**, scholar, W.E.B. DuBois addresses the issue plaguing the African American male. Though written over a century ago, his exposition is highly relevant today. He writes, "From the double life every American Negro must live, as a Negro and as an American, as swept on by the current of the nineteenth while yet struggling in the eddies of the fifteenth century, —from this must arise a painful self-consciousness, an almost morbid sense of personality and a moral hesitancy which is fatal to self-confidence."

I would argue that perhaps an education that reflected more of the African American experience would empower the Black male. Harvard offers the chance to study under top professionals in the field and the opportunity to engage

in intellectual discourse about the state of urban education. The institution's mission to revolutionize and solve significant challenges within education align perfectly with my goals to conquer issues in urban education.

Furthermore, the opportunity to study at an Ivy League University not only diversifies my educational background but also increases my worldliness. Please allow me to take m next *step forward toward bettering myself, so that I, in turn, can help the disenfranchised become productive members of society--one student at at time.*

Needless to say, I was accepted into the School Leadership program in November 2009. I was scheduled to report to Boston, August of 2010. Myriam and I were married May 2010. I had been married to the girl of my dreams for three months and then I was off to Boston to live in campus housing. The second most challenging issue that I had to face was that as a married man, I had to go back and forth to New Jersey to see my wife.

I lived on campus in the Cronkhite Dorms, which were all singles with a communal bathroom and kitchen on the floor. There was a dining hall on the first floor of the building. I felt bamboozled because when I envisioned Harvard, I thought the facilities and amenities were better than Rutgers. I imagined I would be living in a state of the art environment. At minimum, I knew there would be: Central AC system and modern bathrooms. I was sadly mistaken. I lived on my own as a grown man three years prior to actually been accepted, so I had to make major adjustments to my living arrangements. It was worse when Myriam came to visit.

Crimson Epiphany

Just to give you insight, unlike a traditional school where there are a bunch of classes that are considered core requirements, the Harvard Graduate School allows you to take *any* class in the graduate school to fulfill the graduation requirement of 32 credits. My program had two classes that we had to take but all of the other classes were up for grabs. For example, my cohort was required to take a leadership class every Friday for the entire year, but we could take classes at the Kennedy School of Government to complete our graduation requirement.

The work independently wasn't difficult. However, there was a lot of work to cover. In any given class, there were 50-75 articles, 2-4 books, weekly assignments, group work, projects, seminars, and workshops. That was all for one class and we had four or five classes each semester. I was stressed in the beginning as I knew I had to be a husband who was engaged in my wife's life and a student who had to produce exceptional work. I'm like, *Oh my God, this is too much.* There were so many articles and books. I think I probably had a stack of about 300 pages of articles per class that we had to read. On top of that, I had to travel via bus to connect with my wife at least twice a month.

The biggest lesson that I learned initially was that the early bird gets the worm. My program required us to match and pick a principal *prior* to arriving on campus. The faculty sent memos about preparing for the year, but I was just so focused on getting married and doing things with my wife and making sure that the end of the school year procedures were done, that I hardly paid attention to those notifications. As you can imagine, when I got to Harvard I was overwhelmed because I had so much to get done and I wasn't used to that type of freedom. I had to match with a principal of the school while choosing classes for me to take to graduate. I was the second youngest cohort at 26 years old and the only Black male. The youngest cohort was Chris, whom I befriended. His father was the Deputy Governor of Massachusetts back in the 70's. I also became friends with two other guys, John and Josh. It was crazy to *not* hear my classmates talking about school loans or debt. Again, I felt less-than, like I was just trying to trudge through. Harvard prided itself on being a school for the urban community, but some of the things they projected had no validity based on my experiences.

When I shared my sentiments, I got a lot of push-back. I'd look around and give a nod to the Black girls in my class like, "You feel me?" but they didn't respond because they grew up in Alabama or somewhere with two parents in the household. They had a different type of struggle. I connected with a girl named Rajique, who had a very similar lifestyle to mine. Then I became cool with an Asian girl named Betty, who was from the hood. We were able to see eye-to-eye. I used my homegirls as a sounding board. I'd ask them, "Is that the truth? Does that resonate with you?"

I was adamant about showing Harvard who I really was. I joined the Black Student Union and became part of a committee that showed films. I held Harvard accountable to the standards needed to work in the urban community. I selected Black guest speakers and I extended invites to the cohort and talked openly about my struggles. "I'm having a hard time connecting with you guys. I don't think you understand who I am as a person. To help you understand, I'm having this event. Come out." Many of my classmates did come out and were very supportive. To the point that I was elected "Class Marshall." Only one person in the cohort could win that position and this person was able to keep order. I kept order in a different way and I brought flavor to the school. I was able to be myself while obtaining a world-class education, of which I am very proud. I graduated in 2011 with a Degree in School Leadership.

Equal Opportunity Quest

The most challenging thing that I struggled with at Harvard was the race relations. I had to be a principal intern while attending classes. I could feel the tension and awkwardness but could not put it in words. Not to mention the big difference level of discomfort when I had to visit a school. There was such a big difference between high school and elementary school teachers being responsible for the kids. In high school, the kids were pretty much on their own once the final bell rang.

My first role in elementary school was bus duty. It sounds trivial, but it was very important. I thought, how hard can this be? At first, I could not understand why students were being bused all around the city. None of the routes made sense in terms of zoning. In Jersey City, if you live in a certain district then you go that district's public school. No exception, unless you go to private school. I was shocked that in 2011 in

Boston, they were still working on desegregation to integrate students to have more exposure to opportunities. *Didn't the Montgomery Bus Boycott happen in 1965? Did they know about Dr. King and the Civil Rights Movement?* I was totally unaware of Boston's late arrival. There were buses lined up outside and I had to organize students by tables so I could call their bus number to go home. The checks and balance system had to be air-tight because it would have been extremely detrimental to have a student miss his or her bus. I enforced the system to organize the buses, teachers, and students.

In another capacity, I was a leading a group of 4th grade math teachers. There was a lot of dissonance, because the team lead was adamant about showing the principal that she could do it by herself. So naturally the rest of team did not get along with her. We were working them as if it were a typical Professional Development session. All of the teachers were required to bring their quarterly work to be analyzed by a computer program. It is a very effective process. For example, one teacher's results could show that 20 kids got problem number one correct and 20 kids got number three correct. Oftentimes, one teacher could have 90% correct on a problem, while another teacher had only 10% correct. I asked the teachers to reenact what they did, how they explained it, and act it out to help kids better understand the problem. The goal was to infuse collaboration and discussion around "How might this problem work differently?" Teachers had a short time to rehearse. I used this method as a teacher instruction to let them know that as a leader, I am here to help you. It also was a tool to help kids hone in on their skills. I flourished under this type of micromanagement. I have not seen this done before and still haven't. Many of the teachers did well using this method and I use it in charter school with my teachers. This gives true meaning to the phrase "each one teach one."

Although I had only been teaching in middle school, there was a push from within to work on the high school level. As I mentioned, the early bird catches the worm and those principal internship placements were taken. I didn't do my research and was not properly prepared. Not that I was given the leftovers, however, I had slim pickings for my choice of school and principal. Honestly, I thought all participating principals were vetted through a screening process but they weren't. I am not placing blame, I'm just speaking of the shortcomings I had while participating in the program.

Needless to say, the principal I chose, was a novice principal who didn't trust most of his staff. I did not make headway in leading anything substantive because I couldn't get my foot in the door. I struggled those few months because I had an image of what a principal was in my head, and it didn't line up in real life. I had to manage my expectations and not appear overly committed to help. He had issues with relinquishing control, so I was fighting to take over an issue like scheduling or professional development, but to no avail. I asked for a transfer in hopes to have a different experience.

I went back to the list and found an elementary placement. I served as an intern principal at a high school from October - February and switched to elementary K-5 from February until the end of the school year in May. Those experiences were drastically different. Serving as a principal intern for the elementary school made me prioritize my standards. I asked myself, *What's important to you? Who is important to you? Why do you do the work?* I was able to draw a line in the sand at that moment and I realized that I wanted to fulfill my students' expectations.

Odd Man Out

I just remember the first day that I did not wear my wedding ring. I told Myriam I felt like I didn't need to wear it as I was never a fan of the old traditional sense of marriage or wedding bands. Meanwhile, at a reception there was a young lady trying to get with me. I didn't really catch on until towards the end of the event when she stated, "you know, you can come over to my apartment anytime." This was the first time a white woman has ever tried to hit on me at least that I could remember. My wife tells me all the time that a lot of women make passes at me but I don't necessarily see it. Then I realized that I needed to put on my wedding ring because of the 60% to 30% ratio, women to men. I'm not saying that I am a hunk, but some of those women came to get married as well. I wasn't privy to that lifestyle. Needless to say, I wear my wedding ring religiously.

It was déjà vu. I found myself feeling like I did in under-graduate and graduate school - like the outsider because I didn't connect with many of my cohort members. Going to class I felt really disenfranchised. I remember saying, *I don't know how much longer I'm going to do this.* I wanted to give up. The work was a lot. I still had to be a husband and I was trying to figure out who I was as a leader. Even when I went out with my cohorts to pubs in the area, I was the only Black male student in the group and oftentimes in the entire venue. Going to pubs was palpable.

At Rutgers, I went to school with individuals who looked like me or at least I connected with them through common-alities like the same hood. I was the only Black dude in the cohort, so I went to the Black women, thinking that I was go-ing to find solace in them in terms of connection, but many of the ladies although they were not necessarily affluent, they came from a very different and privileged background than I did. For example, one of my friends at Harvard drove a Jaguar. I have never driven Jaguar, let alone knew someone who actually owned one. The eye-opener for me was that not everyone who looks like you has your narrative. In fact, the closest person that I could relate to in terms of similar back-grounds was a woman who grew up in a working-class single parent household. It's great for the culture. She's now a lead-er in the educational sector and I'm elated because I love the redemptive story; started from the bottom now we're here! Turning nothing into something is always the story that I love.

Finding My Groove

Around November, I connected with others by serving on the executive board committee of the Black Student Union. I truly felt connected to those individuals because we understood that we were Black and focused on education. I definitely got my superpowers from those relationships. I had a very good friend who also joined with me and I was able to bounce ideas off of her.

I thrived in social settings and looked forward to making connections with a smorgasbord of Black individuals from different cohorts within the graduate school and other graduate programs. I looked forward to our get-togethers to speak about our versions of being Black. I found peace. Not because it was cool, but being in that environment with the Black Student Union rejuvenated me to want to lead and make change. I wanted to teach non Blacks about life as a Black individual, particularly the Black man.

Within my cohort, I just felt like there was a deficit. Harvard's claim to fame is that they are liberal and teach individuals who wanted to be leaders in urban communities how to effect change through socio academic development. I didn't think that they were as liberal as they claimed to be. Instead, I thought they were very traditional and part of the "systemic" oppression. They had white men teaching Black classes. As much as they try to connect with the community or integrate some of the things that they've gone through into a large idea of liberation and educational equity, it didn't feel genuine because they represented the system of oppression. I had a hard time grappling with some of the ideas they posed in class because I was from an urban community. I also taught in those communities and I had a difficult time subscribing to some of their academic dogma.

I branched out and connected with other people around the Harvard community. I started working on a play that did not materialize. The premise of the play was to have four main characters: An African native, a Puerto Rican in New York, a white guy from Nebraska, and me, a Black guy from Jersey City. The vision I created was to expose some of the racist behavior we experienced while on campus. The four of us met a couple of times and they ended up not feeling it. We were going to perform four different monologues while on stage with a common thread between the four of our experiences. I admit that it was controversial and may have made students and administration uncomfortable, yet it is the primary reason why things have remained the same. Real conversations are not happening in the right settings. I want to be part of the true shift to have these necessary tough conversations with individuals from various ethnicities and backgrounds.

Level Up

The biggest takeaway is that you have to make each growth experience the way that you want it to be. The ultimate lesson is that you have to create the healthy lifestyle that you desire. I was adamant about not allowing a $70,000 Harvard education go to waste. I think oftentimes we attend places of learning and become students as opposed to leaders and teachers. I took the bull by its horns and you should do the same. While at Harvard my grandfather Eugene, the last grandparent died. I had to deal with his death, my marriage, and my outlier feelings as a developing educational leader. I made a decision to stand tall because with so much going on, there was no room for failure.

My Harvard experience solidified who I was supposed to be. Working through those growing pains and managing to rise as a leader among leaders, showed me that if I put my mind to it, I could do anything.

We all were required to make an end-of-the-year presentation which was a culmination of projects from August to May. It was to incorporate everything that we discussed and learned throughout the year. I remember one of my fellow cohort member's presentations vividly because it gave me insight into how others viewed me. This particular guy was the smartest person of our cohort. To give you an idea of his dopeness, there were two awards given during graduation, one went to me for being the Class Marshal and the other went to him for being the smartest in the cohort.

For his culminating project, he had a board with each of the cohort members' names. In the beginning of his presentation, he said, I have a question or comment that I would like to push us on. Those questions were written on the other side of the index card only allowing us to see our names. Basically, we took the cards at our own risk. Because it was the way that the cards were placed on the boards with our names visible, you had to actually grab it and turn it around to see what he said. He's even said grab your card if you choose at your leisure. I was just looking and I just kept thinking to myself, *wow what a cowardly way to tell someone what you think of them without having the repercussions of a face-to-face conversation.* On the back of my card, it read, "Why do you play the victim? Why do you allow others to speak for you?"

That question struck a chord with me because in my head I thought that just sharing my story, which was a triumphant story of my working hard to get out of the hood was one of strength and survival, not victimhood. However, he perceived that the way I showed up in class as victimizing myself as a Black kid from the projects. His comment left a powerful impression on me because I wasn't sure exactly what he was talking about at the time. I didn't want any of my cohorts to feel sorry for me. I wanted to be open and communicate my vantage point. I had been rehearsing the same narrative for so long that I didn't know what else to say. Towards the end of the semester I had some white men wanting to meet me for validation. I left needing to do some soul searching in that regard. This has been a point of reference in my counseling sessions a number of times. Which led to months of counseling around victimizing and what does that look like and areas of my life that I can improve upon.

In Boston, the racial tension that exists there is palpable, especially at the sports events. I felt disenfranchised at Rutgers because of my socio-economic status. However, I felt disenfranchised at Harvard because of the color of my skin. I think it is important that I point that out. To dive further into my reasoning, the director of my program is a white male who I referred to earlier. He is a nice guy, but he is a person claiming to connect with the urban plight but, in my opinion, he didn't and is not capable of doing so. I struggled with my internship placements because I didn't believe I was getting a great experience. I felt like he wasn't supportive.

In his defense, I never felt that he treated me badly because of my race. I believe in hindsight, that he wanted me to be better because of how the world viewed me. He spoke a little about that when we had a heart-to-heart, but I felt like he made several judgments about who I was and my work ethic. I had a very difficult time not attributing his comments to my race as I connected to several cohort members who weren't doing or contributing nearly as much as I was. I eventually saw the dean about my concerns with the director of the program and asked if she could intervene.

During graduation when I won Class Marshal, the program director said very nice things about me when he handed me my diploma. The Class Marshal was awarded to the individual who added to the learning experience to the cohort. The perk was that I led the line with the flag. I stood there to shake the hands of my entire cohort and they called my name last to so-lidify my efforts. Winning the award was a total surprise. So when my cohort referred to me as a victim, I felt that I was jug-gling all of my experiences well. I mean, I dealt with things that he had no clue about because he was a white, straight man.

I found out that a lot of my other friends weren't doing anything significant either, but that they just kept their mouth shut. I didn't really know how to play the game at my young age and many of my cohorts were in their 40s. I felt validat-ed by the whole experience because he was coming at me for some strange reason. Now that I think about it, he came at me because he felt a level of insecurity. Yet I was under the impres-sion that he could relate to me as an individual, as a teacher, and as a leader, but unfortunately, that was not the case.

You +Preparation = the Answer

"Education is the passport to the future, for tomorrow belongs to those who prepare for it today."
Malcolm X

I think that the biggest takeaway from my Harvard experience is that you have to fight for what you believe in. You have to fight for whatever you deem is your truth. I knew what it was like growing up in the urban community, so I didn't need to read a book about it. I didn't need to theorize my experiences as it was a way of life for me.

I was grateful to receive the Class Mashal award, yet I didn't view it as if I'd arrived. However, it definitely solidified that the fight that I fought wasn't in vain. I continue to press for it today because I know that in the fight therein lies healing and growth because of the important stance that you choose to take. You speak your truth and others behind you will be delivered and set free.

I know it sounds cliché, but just believe in yourself. Dr. King was adamant about fighting the good fight of faith. We have to believe as individuals who are not the majority that we are relevant to the larger picture in terms of being considered when decisions are made. We're here, we're not just a number, but we *are* the experience. It's in our best interest to show up so that we subliminally give others permission to do the same.

Harvard saw what Jersey City built. If you're from an urban community and would like to explore Ivy League schools, it is imperative that you don't walk in feeling like you come with a deficit. The survival skills learned while navigating the community has prepared you to take on the world. They are lucky to have experienced individuals in those settings. While at Harvard, I connected with another friend who also grew up in the projects and was pursuing a different graduate degree. The point is, those of us from the hood have what it takes to rise and become leaders in our communities and around the world. Be mindful of the impression you leave on others. Connect and engage with those who are genuine and want to see you succeed. I am thankful for my professor at New Jersey City University for bringing the Harvard opportunity to me, yet I know that Harvard would not have accepted me if I didn't produce. More importantly, I know for a fact that I wouldn't have been able to produce in the manner that I did without my Jersey City community. Thank you for making me the man I am today.

4th Marking Period

THE RETURN: Coming Home/ Coming Full Circle

CHAPTER 8

New Beginnings

As you can see, the bulk of this project is centered around my childhood and teenage years. Those experiences were critical to who I have become as a man and educational leader. All of the lessons learned, trials and triumphs had a scaffolding effect - building upon each other to help me grow. I don't want young people in their hoods to despise their challenging or dysfunctional beginnings, because at the end of the day they make us stronger and wiser.

I chose eight chapters for this book because eight is a significant number in Christianity and other cultures. In the Bible, it means "new beginning" and symbolizes a new order of life. I am at an exciting phase in my life in moving back to my hometown of Jersey City, New Jersey. My wife and I purchased our home and our son AJ has his own room. Growing up, I never had my own room, so AJ is fortunate in that respect. Now if we could only get him to stay in there, that would be great.

Another point about the number eight is that in Asian cultures, it is believed to be the totality of the universe and represents wealth and prosperity. Mathematically, if you lay an eight on its side, you have the infinity symbol. Eight is also the key to one of the most famous mathematical formulas: The Fibonacci Sequence. Each number in the sequence is the sum of the two numbers that precede it. For math geeks like me, the sequence goes: 0, 1, 1, 2, 3, 5, 8, 13, 21, 34, to infinity. The mathematical equation describing it is $Xn+2= Xn+1 + Xn$. I hope you appreciate that I saved one math problem for the end. I honestly could not resist.

Working with numbers and improving the educational system in urban communities are my driving force. I remember reading books about the teacher strike in Newark and Jersey City. I was moved by the teachers who had a personal vested interest in their students by living in the same community. They shopped at the same stores, ate at the same restaurants, and attended the same events as their students. I remember saying to myself, *I need to take a personal account as well.* I wish more teachers would take onus of this as well. It is important to build a connection with the kids and have shared experiences. Even if you don't live in that city where you work, you have the same experiences. When students hurt, I hurt. When students are happy, I'm happy. I want to see these kids thriving. I am proud that I am from Jersey City. I got what I needed and now I'm back!

Called

*"There are two great days in a person's life -
the day we are born and the day we discover why."*
William Barclay

Shortly thereafter, my friend Shelly, whom I grew up with in Jersey City was the principal of a high school. I was interviewing for teaching postions and had a few offers to choose from. Shelly also offered me a teaching position at her school. I declined because my salary was not in her budget. She called me back two weeks later and said, "I can match what you want." "Let's make history!" I shouted. I admire her because I know where she came from and we've always supported one another.

I teach math and currently serve as a Crisis Intervention Teacher with the Jersey City Board of Education. As a teacher, I have to pull from multiple resources in order to get my students attention. When they are listening to music, I ask them to let me hear it and pose questions about the artists. I look at their magazines, visit their homes, and stay connected to them. My purpose is to reach them where they are.

When I teach, I want to be relevant. Kids love to dance and there was a popular song, *You Can't Wu-tang Better Than Me* that I used to teach a lesson on parallelograms and rectangles. The dance applicability to the math lesson started in public school. The goal was for kids to know the difference between a parallelogram and other geometric shapes. The kids stand and move their arms back and forth and left and right. We figured out the angles of the shapes and then dance and sing the definitions of the shapes. These types of lessons are fun and are connected to the learning objective.

The Motherland Experience

The more I interact with my students, the more I think about my amazing experience teaching high school in South Africa. I applied to the program online and attended a mandatory meeting at Columbia University. The main criteria for acceptance was that you had to demonstrate how the constituents in South Africa could benefit from your expertise. More importantly, how your methods and ideas for leading can bring positive transformation. I went to South Africa in the Summer of 2014.

When people think of Africa, they have a tendency to picture Somalis with flies buzzing around their nostrils. Going to South Africa was a true revelation. I was able to hear from true Africans what life is really like. My Blackness was validated and viewed as beautiful. I understood that slavery was the culprit of African-Americans failing to recognize themselves in a positive light. The journey was spiritual, authentic, and allowed me to understand my feelings.

As Americans, spirituality was given to us through religion. In Africa, spirituality *is* in their living. They *know* God and are zealous for Him. Capitalism isn't on the agenda because they don't understand it. It's like a caste system. Wherever you're born, that's where you're going to die. You take an exam and your grade determines your major. Although materialism is not a chief concern, the people in the areas I visited didn't look poverty-stricken, yet they had minimal possessions.

A major contrast between American and African society is that Americans' validation comes from what we possess or how we look. It's the complete opposite for Africans. I saw what Americans would consider to be an unattractive woman with bald spots at a workshop I attended. In America, she would have been ostracized. I was shocked at the people's response to her. She shared a poem and the people loved on her tremendously. Love was predicated and not her appearance or status.

I connect with women through teaching, and as a result, I see the cattiness among them. During one of our teaching seminars, there was a woman who arrived late. She was gorgeous. Her presence took over the room once she entered. I initially thought people didn't speak to her because they were jealous of her. After the session, the teachers rode home in a van; three men and six women, including the gorgeous woman. After the woman exited the van, the women started marveling over her, "She's beautiful. She has it going on." They were praising her for at least one minute! I can't imagine the women in my school in Jersey City praising an attractive woman like that.

My assignment in South Africa was two-fold: (1) assist the principal with daily responsibilities; and (2) support teachers and help them develop. The principal of the school taught trigonometry and I shadowed him. I hadn't done higher order math in years. We got to using proofs and geometry terminology. As I was writing on the board, I heard a few boys talking. I turned around swiftly so I could reprimand those who were talking. To my surprise, the other boys were actually helping a student who was struggling.

One thing that was daunting was the young people's fascination with American culture. They knew all the celebrities and were eager to find out more about them. "Do you know Jay-Z?" they inquired. "Yeah, he lives right next door to me. Of course not!" I joked. I did have to check them on sagging their pants because that is a style that I don't think any culture should be proud of.

The teachers in South Africa were as young as 18 and 19 years old. They started out as Teacher Assistants and moved into teaching. One day I had to present and speak about a procedure that I wanted them to focus on. Whenever I am getting ready to present, my body reacts physiologically; I feel like I need to use the bathroom. Whenever there's food, I'm usually first in line. I hadn't eaten since the morning and there were hoagies for lunch. A girl walked over to me and said, "Go ahead and miss your blessings." It was a chastisement for being gluttonous. It was also an eye-opener. My focus was on being satisfied. I had put six hoagies on my plate and ate two.

There was another occasion in which I had a few minutes to get from one class to another. I went to the bathroom first.

Running water is scarce in a lot of places in South Africa. I had put soap on my hands and the water was coming out like, "drip, drip, drip." I started to panic. I thought the kids were going to run out of the class. It made me realize that I needed to stop and wash my hands for sanitary reasons. We do so much with our hands, like opening doors, shaking hands and carrying bags that we should take better care of them. Little things like running water made me conscience of the fact that I was in a world far away from what I was accustomed to.

As part of my assignment, we were divided up into teams where we conducted workshops on co-teaching and how to develop background knowledge. We gave the teachers time to practice because they had no clue as to what was required of them. Our team tested different groups of schools, teachers, and leaders to help them be better educators for their students. They were very receptive and open to what my team brought to the table. Whenever I do workshops, I make sure that I am emulating exactly how I want it done. We act it out co-teaching and one-on-one sit-downs by doing the same lesson we presented. By the end of the program, two South African teachers were doing what we taught.

I built strong relationships and connected with the natives. I spent the night in their homes instead of the bed and breakfast that was provided in the program. Although they did not have much, most lived in one room, they were willing to share what little they had with me. Their acts of kindness and generosity struck a chord and birthed Kismet of Kings. I work with that same mantra: I do not have a lot, but whatever I have I am willing to share with others. I am proud of my contribution to the people in the community of Diepsloot, South Africa and I hope to return soon.

Standing A Million Feet Tall

Growing up hearing the barber shop stories when the guys came back from the Million Man March, on October 16, 1995, made me feel like I had missed out on a momentous Black moment. I was too young to attend but watched parts of it in school in Mr. Howard's class. However, two years later, on October 16, 1997, marked as The Day of Atonement by Minister Farrakhan, I was selected to speak at the march in Newark. Actually, myself and one other student were selected to speak from our Saturday morning science and math club at P.S. 14. I enjoyed those extra classes and I think the instructors were also conscious about teaching us the ropes to be productive citizens. They presented facts on eating healthy, how to meditate, and how much water to drink. The head of the program was brother Rockman. He was connected to my teacher Ms. Newsome. There were about 500 people in attendance, but it felt like 1000. I remember sitting there and hearing people go up and say, "No justice no peace!" Each person spoke of their idea of what freedom looked like for our people. Most spoke of empowerment and how education was the key. We did not go to school that Saturday day and I was literally practicing my speech for weeks. My turn was

coming up and my nerves were shot. Everyone was supportive and said things like "Go on brother, say that!" I did not
know how to ad lib and just went through my speech without
giving much eye contact. My mom and those in the community were proud of me. Especially when a candid photo of me
at the event was in the newspaper.

Fast forward to October 2015 for the 20 year Anniversary
of the Million Man March. I was adamant about not missing
this historic event on the mall of Washington, D.C. It was a
full circle moment because I was now in the education sector
and bringing a mentor, Larry, with me. At that time, I was the
Dean of Instruction at Foundation Academy Charter School
and I had built close relationships with parents and students.
It is at this school that birthed my constituents for Kismet
of Kings. Larry's mom was very protective and she was con-
cerned with the overnight trip. He was a promising student
and ultimately the hope for the family, which I totally understood.

Larry's mom agreed. We loaded the car with me, Larry
and four of my boys. We were listening to Kendrick Lamar,
Drake, The Weekend, Rihanna, hip hop and R&B. Most of the
conversations were loud with arguing back and forth with
such strong discourse about which fast food is better, McDon-
ald's or Burger King, and other brand comparisons. Larry sat
there taking it all in. I apologized for my loud friends. It was
very interesting because for a moment I was embarrassed. I
was Mr. Spears with this Harvard background and now I am in

the car kickin' it with my boys and I'm just "Lewis" in Larry's eyes.

We arrived at our hotel early so we decided to grab a bite to eat. This was also the first time Larry was able to see me plan our day. For starters, what we were going to eat, how much time we would spend there and what we would do after the Washington Mall. He got to see me in my element if you will; just chillin'. We stopped at Burger King because we dare not stop at McDonalds!

Afterward, we headed to the Washington Mall to check things out. I had never seen so many people gathered in one place. Outside of my South Africa experience, I had never witnessed so much brotherly love from Christians and the Nation of Islam. We kept moving closer toward the stage in order to really hear the speakers. I saw a light in Larry's eyes. He is quiet but very powerful. I really like this kid. There was the smell of incense in the air and this overwhelming feeling of love. In that crowd of people, you constantly heard, "So sorry my brother," or "So sorry my sister." Then we got to hear Minister Farrakhan speak about collective economics; "if you love yourself you would not hurt your brother." He also spoke about things happening in your community that should be important to us and how powerful we are.

Then as we were taking it all in, I passed by a woman and said hi. She turned and said, "Lewis Spears how are you?" I could not believe my eyes. It was my elementary school teacher Ms. Newsome! She was in her hijab so she could not give me a long hug. We exchanged numbers and spoke about my friend Shelly who was a school principal. Ms. Newsome is Muslim and introduced me to the Nation of Islam. She showed me a lot about that world. I told Larry that this moment was something really dope because she was my teacher who taught me about the Million Man March. It was an amazing full circle moment.

We went to dinner that night and my boys went out for drinks. I stayed behind with Larry because I had to be like a responsible parent to him. Myriam had not had AJ, but all I kept thinking about is that I wanted Larry to be safe. God forbid if something would have happened to that young man. I would be at a loss. I felt restricted that night but in a good way.

On the ride back to New Jersey the next morning it felt good to be a part of the event. There was a sense of pride as my boys and I hadn't heard anything new, but it reinforced what we had been saying to young men. The experience was a great conversation starter for Larry and my other students. So now on the ride back, we *did not* play music. Instead, we talked about the deaths of Freddie Gray, Trayvon Martin and the Walter Scott shooting in Charleston, South Carolina. We were angry at the disrespect to people of color and how we need to focus on developing the shift in the narrative and the negative stereotypes.

I remember feeling satisfied and complete. The camaraderie and connecting to the bigger picture that I am bigger than myself as a community was real. We left Washington,

D.C. with a stronger desire to help each other and be intentional about developing others.

Boyz to Men

I didn't understand my stepdad Kenny as a boy, but as a man, I have a better perspective and appreciation for who he is. We're closer now that he and my mother are separated. I was critical of him my entire life, not because he wasn't my biological father, but because I thought he was incredibly selfish. In retrospect, I find myself giving him more credit where it's due. He definitely stepped up after I lost my father. When his mother passed away last November, Myriam and I were away in Mexico, so he went and stayed with my mom. When we returned, Mommy got herself together and made sure she was there for him. They cooked together this past Thanksgiving. They've developed a really good friendship. They're even closer than when they were together. Kenny's still in love with Mommy. He makes sure she's good and she takes advantage of that expression of kindness.

Ladies First

Last, but certainly not least, a few words about my wife and my mother. My mother will always be "Regina Spears White" as she loves to proclaim. Her defense, which makes my skin crawl is "I could've been a drunk and I coulda did all that you said I did, but I always put my kids first and then I used whatever money I had left over and I did *that*!" In reality, my mother never had any money left over. There was no such thing because she didn't save money. We weren't going on family vacations. At the end of the day, my response is always, "OK, Mom." We had a heart-to-heart recently and she said some things that I didn't expect to hear. "I don't like the impression that some people have of me, like, 'Oh, that's Gina, don't mess with Gina, you know she's crazy!" I always thought that my mother acted like that so people would know they couldn't mess with her. Now she sounds embarrassed by it. "Why they keep saying that about me?" I couldn't help but laugh. "Mom, come on. You can't be mad about that. If you want to change it, that's another thing." "But why they keep saying, 'Lewis, you better get your mother!' What the heck *you* gon do?" she asked angrily. Ironically, I'm the only one who can calm my mother down. "Mom, you know I can't tackle you or anything. We have a friendship." "You right," she said softly. It was weird to hear that my mother was worried about what others thought about her. I almost felt like saying, "Well, what did you expect?" My sister Kamiesha will hit me up and say, "Lewis, come get Mommy. She's goin' crazy." She keeps me posted on my mother's business as well, so I know what's really going on.

Myriam and my mother's relationship has improved a lot. Myriam knows how to handle her. She'll just say, "Anh-ah Gina" or "Knock it off." My mother was about to give my nephew some beer. Myriam scolded her, "You know you shouldn't be doing that. Knock it off!" They're in that comfortable place now. Myriam had to be herself. She was intimidated at first.

Who wouldn't be? I think her only pet peeve is that my mother is a smoker. Myriam gets so annoyed with her that you just see her cringing, but Mommy doesn't care.

The irony of forever being connected to these two amazing women is that on the surface you would think that they are the complete opposite of each other. Myriam is a prim and proper physician and my mother is a no holds barred "physician" whenever she wants to be. My mother will always be the type of person who walks into a room, knocks everything over, causes a raucous, and doesn't realize it. Myriam walks into a room and fixes everything she thinks is out of order. My mom is up front and in your face. Myriam is reserved and you will know how she feels about a situation a few days later.

Despite their differences, their similarities speak to their core values. Both are very courageous women. If Myriam wants something, she goes after it, so does my mom. They are both family oriented and would do anything for her unit to survive and thrive. Myriam is adamant about making family sacrifices even as a physician working lots of hours per week. Now that I am older I think I'm becoming a Mama's boy. I just get in these moods where I want to be around her, eating home cooked turkey wings, macaroni and cheese, and collard greens. When I'm finished stuffing my face and talking about everything under the sun, I'm in better shape to face the world. Through it all, the elephant the room is that they both love me and they have the ability to love, connect, and ride or die support to the end. Both are beautiful, amazing, and are transformative in their own right. I know that I am blessed to have them in my life.

You + Service to Others = The Answer

Kismet Awaits

Kismet = destiny or fate

When I look back over my life at this point, I see myself as the rose that grew from concrete that Tupac so eloquently spoke of in that track with Nikki Giovanni. "Long live the rose that grew out of the concrete when no one else even cared." The significance of such a phenomenon is the fact that a person can survive such a tumultuous process and still be beautiful on the inside and out. Take a look at the kids in our society and all the challenges they have to go through. They may be bruised, they may have some blemishes, but the fact that they've made it through hardships is enough reason to figure out how we can support them and build them up where they are. The fact that I was able to overcome the generational curses of alcoholism, domestic violence, and criminal behavior gives me hope that others can overcome the negative circumstances given to them.

There's nothing this world can throw at you that you can't sustain, as long as you have a made up mind to persevere. This is a call to society. We're able to understand it when it's wrapped up in the package of African kids or third-world countries, but we don't understand it when it's in our own backyard. I always ask questions like, *Is it easier to deal with these issues abroad than it is at home? Is it easier to handle because you're removed or do you really not see it?* The history of slavery makes it easier for society to overlook issues in the Black community and fail to recognize them as important. The consensus becomes, "Whatever predicament they're in, they did it to themselves."

That burns me up. I have a high tolerance for opposing views, but uttering words like this takes me there, I could go in on that. We talk about the mistreatment of our culture. It's as if we're all disposable like we're not even needed. We're massively incarcerated. Law enforcement believes they can kill us and it's OK. Why has it become the norm for a trained professional to kill an unarmed teen because of his manner of dress?

I attended a workshop with a guy who was from Newark but doesn't live there anymore. He was saying, "I don't even shop in Newark. When you go into the stores, those Black people are so rude!" *Do you hear yourself?* I wondered. It's that self-racism, self-loathing that angers me. I asked him, "When was the last time you were in Newark?" "It's been years now. You have to watch your back," he replied. *How did he even know what's happening then?* "I'm in Newark every other day. It's not like that, that's not my experience," I stated. His claims were only further perpetuating ignorance and feeding into the negative stereotypes that Blacks in the hood are a lost cause.

One of the reasons why I founded the non-profit organization, Kismet of Kings is because I wanted to show the young men in the inner city that they have the opportunity to be more than what they see each day. I wanted to be that living example for them to see if I made it, so can you. I want to impart all that I have learned about getting ahead and access to opportunities to help them grow. I want the young men who come through Kismet of Kings to always remember words like equity, restorative justice, love, compassion, fairness, loyalty and other really life-changing concepts to think of what they learned at Kismet of Kings.

I want my young men and all young men to know the true essence of masculinity. It's not about wearing your pants to the ground or disrespecting women but it's about taking on responsibilities that set you apart from the negative stereotypes. It's about developing your community, it's about showing up in the world when it counts.

One of the most important aspects that the Black community must become educated in is investing. Many families don't have life insurance, houses or tangibles to leave as an inheritance so that our kids don't have to start from the bottom. We need to teach our kids to do something productive when they receive money. For example, what would it take to do group economics, such as a sou-sou in the Black community to kick-start people's dreams?

We did presentations about the stock market and financial freedom in urban communities. We were all black and in our 30's. We met once a month and hosted events through-out the year. The purpose was to educate our people about setting themselves and their posterity up for success.

In my space, I see math all around me. Numbers don't lie and with the mounting negative numbers reflecting members of the Black community as it relates to education, crime, and incarceration, I want to flip the script and change those num-bers into positives, one community at a time. Even with all my accolades, I am still not satisfied. There are so many things on my to-do list as it relates to my family and serving those around me. My mom and my therapist asked me will I ever be satisfied. My answer is "I hope so, but I just don't know, because life has so many infinite possibilities."

Photo Memories

My first birthday. Sittin' on top of the world...or just my mom's bed.

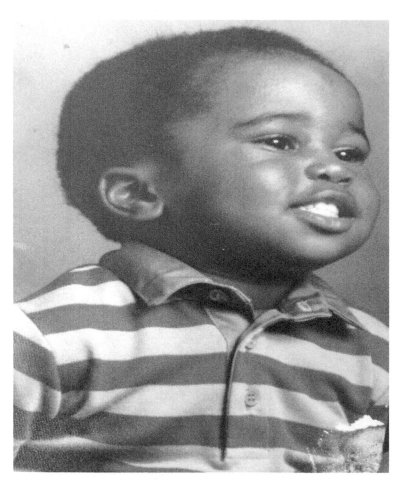

Chubby Cheeks!

My son AJ. My pride and joy.

Definitely!

High school, circa 1999. I always wore a Black leather jacket to make me look cool. Peer Leadership was always important to me.

My brother (holding cousin Tymir), Cousin Javon, my grandfather Eugene Spears, Jalil Spears, and me.

Liberated Gospel Choir, Rutgers University, 2002. Me, Myriam (above), Brittany, Korin, and Esere.

Myriam and I at an arcade. Rutgers University, 2004.

Our engagement photo, 2009.

Our wedding day, May 7, 2010!

It's official...Dr. Myriam Spears! Graduation from Rowan University
School of Osteopathic Medicine, May 2010.

*On safari in Limpopo, South Africa to visit Kruger
National Park, July 2013.*

Putting in the work. Harvard University, 2011.

Thanks to my boy Joshua who hooked it up for me to meet Carolyn Kennedy. Harvard University, Kennedy School, 2011,

Harvard School of Leadership Graduation day, 2011.
Program Class Marshal.

Our first annual Kismet of Kings Take Charge of Your Destiny event.
Media captured me tying a young man's tie.

Guest speakers for our Take Charge of Your Destiny Event, 2014. Pastor Carlos Perez (left), Dr. Alex Ellis (center), and me.

Myriam and me, Black tie affair, 2015.

Thanks to sponsorship to Kismet of Kings, our young men were treated to a Jets game, 2016.

*Actor, Coley Speaks, a fellow Booker T. Washington Project's alumni,
attended our Take
Charge of Your Destiny event, 2017.*

Actor, Mack Wild, supporting our Take Charge of Your Destiny Event, 2017.

Original Black Wall Street of Jersey City, NJ, circa 2018. (L-R) Mr. Whitehall, Gillian Sargeant-Allen, Noreen, Venus Smith and me.

A Six Flags rendering to make you smile, 2004. Always remember that love is what love does :)

ACKNOWLEDGMENTS

Your belief in me made me finesse this project with effica-cy, Coach! Kim Rouse, thank you is not enough! Armando, my therapist turned friend! Thanks for helping me to live a better version of myself daily. Your (spiritual) guidance has helped me to that, no, I'm not crazy lol, but that I have to work diligently to make things happen for myself! Look, I did IT! Reading this I know you are going to hear your influence and see how your impact in my life has made THE DIFFER-ENCE ...saying thank you isn't enough.

You've been more than a photographer, you have cap-tured the best moments of my life. I appreciate you for all that you've done and continue to do! Big ups to you, James Anthony! My guy, Stephen Reid, came through as well. Thanks for the cover!

Uncle Robert, Aunt Eileen, Aunt Ruthann and Uncle Frank for being the pillars, the goalposts for us to follow. I pay hom-age to you with this body of work. It gives me great pleasure that you will be able to read my interpretation of the life you helped to create for me. Seeing you in action at family func-tions makes me miss GRUM more than you will ever know. I do not know where I'd be without your sacrifices.

My godmother, Lois Borroum, I love and appreciate your wisdom over the years. I appreciate our talks and the ways you have pushed me to be better.

I'm grateful for our relationship and your new role as Pop Pop. Kenny, I appreciate the long talks and new revelations I am getting by connecting with you. In my adult life, our relationship has flourished the most. I am sincerely honored to call you, POPS!

My INFLUENCERS! My 2nd mothers! I thank you for your conversations, your stories, your trips, your songs, your fights, your love, your flavor, your style, your excursions, your influence. I hope you see the levels of influence you have in my story. I love each of you dearly, my aunts: Betty, Rose, Diane, Lorraine, Kim, Bernice, Sheranda, Tracey, Michelle, Jill, Kamiesha, Margaret, Yolanda, and Dora. A special tribute to Aunt Deloris, who's in heaven now, for how special I felt because of your love. Those trips to *Mumbles* will forever be etched in my memories.

Thank you to my uncles for being a strong force. My uncles are heroes because they take very good care of my aunts. You showed me day-to-day responsibility and what it means to be sacrificial agents for your family. My Uncles: Vernon, Rodney, and Morris!

The bone of my bone, flesh of my flesh! We've experienced so much together and I want you to know that none of that was for naught! That we are going to make history with each of our talents that will influence the world. Thank you for being patient with me especially when I acted like your dad! Lol. It was all out of love. Now that I'm your brother again, I look forward to us building a solid connection. I love you forever, Kayvon, Kamiesha, Alicia!

Since the beginning, I knew no difference! You're my Bonus Siblings: Taeasia, Keith, Shakira, Jabar, Derrick, and Dynia. I love each of you for being a consistent agent of love in my life. I know we do not communicate often, but just know that it's all LOVE.

You're part of my legacy. You're not just my nieces and nephews, you're ME, you're my future! I love you all dearly and remember, there's nothing that you can't do because you are royalty. I hope you view me as someone to look up to. Sending a special shout out to Aziyonah, Yasir, Yamira, Kiyon, Aviana, KJ, Kiara, Tyasia, Jynese, Braxton, Rubie, Seven, Jamiyah, Tymir, Zion, Amorah, Emony, Jada, Jaeonna, Jalil, Amasia, Jasani, Jermaine Jr, King, Rahmir, Ricardo Jr, Jaden, Ihsaan, HoneyBee, BamBam, Izhyr, Jasiah, Gabrielle, Grace, Grayson, Noah and Savannah.

Cousins are your first friends! My cousins are Tiffany, Tamika, Javon, Jalil, Patricia, Shalique, Briana, Sade, Crystal, Morgan, Alexis, Joel, Ryan, Beatrice, Sean, Keith, Derek, Mali, Quan, Tiana, Jared, Jaylin, Chhara, Leon, Dionte... I love you. You are a part of my story because you probably put me in awkward situations and/or we endured them together, lol. We share the same blood and we have the same ability to take on the world. Let us do this together! I am ALWAYS here no matter what! Shout out to my extended family as well.

Without your continuous support and help, my dreams wouldn't be actualized. I appreciate you more than you know. You've brought your love, energy, sweat, blood, and tears into this effort and I am humbly thankful for you. Without you, none of the work we do in Jersey City would be possible. We have so much to more to do so let us get ready for the ride. My illustrious team, Kismet of Kings FAM: Monica, Johanna, Damien, Cameron, Eric, Tariq, Angela, Shauna, Ally, Chantal, Ibn, James, Tameka, Judy, Monique, Letia, and Sonia. I love you!

You are more than friends, you are my family! Words cannot express what you've done for me in this lifetime. It's not about the time, it's about the influence that you have on who I am as an individual. I wouldn't be who I am without you. My Longtime hitters, my A1 Day 1's: Eliud, Shavonne, Sharifah, Hanifah, Sean, Korriese, and Nira.

They say that you're a conglomerate of the five people you surround yourselves around. Good thing I have a smart, caring, goal-oriented and innovative group of individuals who are in my life. We chill together, we break bread together, we laugh, we argue, we make meaning, we analyze, we cook, we connect and everything in between. When I reflect on life and think about the reasons why I am who I am today, YOU are the reasons! My lifelines, my friends: Janine (ACE), Brandy (THE CREATIVE GENIUS), Ricardo, Sharm, Tarik, Atrice, Jason,

Nyrva, Clarence, Martha, Latiek, Tanisha (FAVE), Chawanda (Five Minutes), Sekinah, Mike E., Mike S., Alexis, John, Kim, Josh, Cathey, Brigitte, Elena, Betty, Sarah, Delvon, Juwanna, Eddie, Cassia, Brian, Phil, Mahdi, Corey, Danira, Esere, Chris, Jacquetta, Rosie, Dave (Barber), Kenya, Yardley, Kemini, Amir F., Joseph Jr. (BIL), Ginie (SIL), Bado, CP, Madelyn, Jim, Amro, Bers, Franda, Nicole (Nikki Volvo), Jorques, Ayana, Roberto, and Jon.

Before AJ, I lived to make sure you were good. Although, its different having AJ, I have the same goal. Just know, I'm never too far away. My Godkids: Jiree, Takeya, Ka'liyah, Kai, Nyjeema, DJ, Trey, Terrell, Devin, and Elijah are GOLDEN!

Working side-by-side with you daily has enhanced my life as a teacher, mentor, husband, and friend. I love you and your family so much! So MUCH! We are more than friends and family. Shout out to my Co-Teachers who turned family: Donna (Patrick, Sophia), Crystal (Benorce and Jaden) and Eileen (David, Jailene, Bellz).

These young people helped me to have meaning in life. Continue to show up in the world authentically. There's nothing that you can't do. There are people who are going to be box you in with labels, just know that you can defy all odds stacked against you. You have the ability to weather any storm. I've been strategic about influencing your life in a certain way because I need you all to know that you're worth it. Join in the quest to make this place better than how you found it. My Mentees are the best!!! God is with you! Big ups to Van, Denzel, Rafi, Justin, Isaiah, Maurice, Tamer, Gabriel, Rommel, Thyquel, Jason, Peter, Dwayne, Larry, and Foday.

When I needed an answer to life's issues? Thank YOU! When I was confused about decisions to make? Thank YOU! When I needed direction in life? Thank YOU! Simply put, Thank you for all of your guidance and support. Please take a bow, you deserve it. My mentors/teachers/friends: Mr. Howard, Ms. Landing, Alonso III, Dana, Mr. Gadsden, The Ellis', The Searights, Craig Brown, Gillian, Venus, Noreen, LaQuetta, Tyrone, Alisa, Jerry, Mr. Walker, Gekson, Kabili, Pam, MIchele, The Wallers, and The Hines.

I have to give a special shout out to Mrs. Thomas, Mrs. McMillan, Ms. Elsie, Mrs. Robinson, Mrs. McNeil, and the Dingle Family. I would like to acknowledge my guardian angels in the form of grandmothers: Mrs. Bradford and Mrs. Todd. Without your love and guidance, so early on, my transition into adulthood would have been tough. You both taught me about my life as a Christian in the world.

ABOUT THE AUTHOR

A firm believer in a community pulling itself up by its boot-straps, Lewis Spears has devoted his life and career to manifesting this philosophy. Lewis is no stranger to the ills that plague Jersey City. Having been born and raised in the Booker T. Washington Projects, he saw, first-hand how a lack of education, direction, and mentorship negatively impacts one's quality of life. Determined to change the narrative and break generational and institutional curses, he embarked on a journey to uplift his community by transforming lives-one young person at a time.

After college, his decision to return to his hometown was intentional. He had a deep desire to evoke change from the ground up and invest in Jersey City's challenged school district. For nearly a decade, he has taught across grade levels, focusing primarily on developing the special education population and providing access to up-to-date curriculum with little to no assistance. Education has always been a top priority for Lewis. He was educated in the JCPS and then went on to receive his B.A. from Rutgers University. Lewis continued his formal education at New Jersey City University, receiving a Masters of Arts in Urban Education to enhance his teaching pedagogy. It was at this juncture, that he realized that leadership was the solution to organizational change. In his pursuit to become an educational leader and increase his influence, Lewis attained an Educational Masters in School Leadership from Harvard University. While attending Harvard, he was honored as the Class Marshal, an esteemed award given for exemplary Scholarship in Action, excellent critical-thinking skills, and academic excellence.

Lewis is committed to effecting change by instilling value in the lives of young men in Jersey City and beyond. As a conscious instructor, child advocate and effective leader, Lewis aims to share his talents with anyone aspiring to defy mediocrity. Lewis is the Founder and President of Kismet of Kings, Inc. This enterprise provides a constructivist approach to developing good character. The curriculum highlights prominent Black/Latino men who made significant contributions to the world and utilize their knowledge through project-based learning. Through this organization, an initiative evolved, "Take Charge of Your Destiny," an annual event that he spearheads, challenges young men to reach for greatness. The ultimate goal is to connect young men of color to positive, productive men, in the community who they can emulate.

Lewis was afforded the opportunity to travel abroad and teach in Johannesburg, South Africa, through the Teach With Africa program. Through this endeavor, he was able to deliver a fresh perspective that will continue to stimulate human potential despite environmental challenges. He has taken lessons learned while in South Africa to provoke teachers and students alike, to take a deeper look internally and externally to promote authentic living and communal responsibility. A future goal is to work with the Global Teachers Institute, housed in South Africa, to facilitate travel for young men in urban environments and complete projects in an international setting.

Lewis is passionate about enlightening the next generation and takes great pride in fostering positive connections and providing endless support. Currently, he works as a Crisis Intervention Teacher with the Jersey City Board of Education where he is committed to improving how education is executed on a daily basis. He is the recipient of the Elijah Hendon Award, National Action Network award, and the Distinguished Gentlemen Award. He is currently the 2019 New Leaders Council Fellow for the New Jersey chapter.

Lewis is grounded in his faith and is an active member of his church community. He is happily married to Dr. Myriam Spears and a proud dad to AJ. He is committed to building their family while continuing to create a legacy of upward mobility and service.

Contact Information

Lewis Spears
2014315464
lspears@kismetofkings.org
kismetofkings.org

Facebook: Lewis Spears
Instagram: mrlewisspears
Twitter: LewisSpears5

CONTACT

For bookings and more information log on to:
www.thehoodtoharvard.com

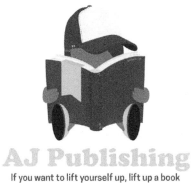

AJ Publishing

If you want to lift yourself up, lift up a book

Made in the USA
Monee, IL
26 October 2020